Theology
and the
Option for the Poor

John O'Brien

D1218169

A Michael Glazier Book
THE LITURGICAL PRESS
Collegeville, Minnesota

THEOLOGY AND LIFE SERIES

Volume 22

Dedicated to my parents
—and to the people of Fatima Mansions
Dublin 8, Ireland

Cover design by David Manahan, O.S.B.

Cover photo: Star Tribune—Minneapolis/St. Paul

A Michael Glazier Book published by The Liturgical Press

1   2   3   4   5   6   7   8   9

Library of Congress Cataloging-in-Publication Data

O'Brien, John.
    Theology and the option for the poor / by John O'Brien.
        p.   cm. — (Theology and life series ; v. 22)
    Includes bibliographical references.
    ISBN 0-8146-5787-7
    1. Poor—Religious aspects—Christianity—History of doctrines.
I. Title. II. Series.
BV639.P6027 1992
261.8'3456—dc20   91-44462
                                      CIP

Contents

Foreword

It seems relatively easy to make useful generalizations about such matters as theological method and the option for the poor. Problems set in when one tries to interpret, explain, and apply in detail what those generalizations might entail. I highly commend John O'Brien's book because of his ability to develop matters at the level both of generalizations and of particular detail.

Father O'Brien brings a wealth of reading to this study. His knowledge of foreign languages has put him in direct touch with sources in Italian, Portuguese, and Spanish, instead of being restricted to French and German as many English-speaking theological scholars still are. Furthermore, over the years his work has taken him to several parts of our world where huge segments of the population live in radical poverty. His personal experience gives an authority to this book that no depth of academic learning can provide by itself.

This book not only maintains an eminently valuable dialogue with the other scholars but also is rooted in years of lived solidarity with the poor of this world. I am glad to be associated with this work and the case it argues.

Gregorian University   Gerald O'Collins, S.I.
Rome

Introduction

It is probably fair to say that the most important as well as the most controversial issue in contemporary Christian theology is what has become known as "the option for the poor." The passions it arouses extend far beyond the visible boundaries of the people of God. To some—usually the weak and voiceless and those who have sided with them—it raises the hope of a renewed humanity in an egalitarian and fraternal world. To others—usually the wealthy and the powerful and those who feel they can find security by serving their interests—it seems to conjure up the specter of revolutionary upheaval and the destruction of the institutions they cherish. To many it remains a slogan, at best partially understood and often deliberately misrepresented.

Within the Church, the debate has, at times, been no less heated, and this, when one considers the implications of taking the "option for the poor" seriously, is perfectly understandable. For if, as a theologian like Jon Sobrino would argue, this option implies forming the Church on the basis of the poor as the structural principle of its organization and mission, then the implications of such an option are enormous. They would include radically different priorities in the allocation of resources and personnel, an alternative decision-making process privileging the voiceless, and a training program for aspirant leaders and pastoral workers as well as religious and priests that emphasized actual participation in the struggle of the poor. It would, moreover, mean significantly modifying the accepted methods of faith reflection. Since the faith that seeks understanding in theology is a faith that impels us to take the side of the poor, making an option for the poor becomes a privileged interpretative standpoint from which to further understand this faith.

Y. Congar developed the notion of *réception* to explain how the destinaries of a text become the coauthors of its expanded meaning, which is the basis of the possibility of a tradition. No text, not even the Scriptures, can yield its meaning of itself. It does so through tradition, which is the presence of the Holy Spirit in communities of thinking, acting believers. When, in partial fulfillment of John XXIII's prayer for a new Pentecost, Vatican II promulgated the text of *Gaudium et spes,* it set the agenda for Catholic theology to engage itself in a direct way with the great contemporary issues facing humankind. For historical and organizational reasons, Vatican II was rather irenic and unduly optimistic in the way it faced many of these issues. When, in a most significant example of what Congar would have called *réception, Gaudium et spes* was "received" by European political theologians and, more significantly still, by Latin American liberation theologians actively involved in the struggle of the poor, a new theological method was born. The pastoral practice that lay at the base of this theological renewal was endorsed at the CELAM conferences of Medellín and Puebla, whose calls to all Christians to make a "preferential option for the poor" have permanently reshaped the theological landscape. This teaching was further endorsed by the Congregation for the Doctrine of the Faith—somewhat hesitantly, one suspects—in *Libertius nuntius* (August 1984) and—rather more generously—in *Libertatis conscientia* (March 1986). As a result of the impulse from the CELAM conferences, this pastoral practice became the springboard for a theological renewal; and the theological trend, which was already tentatively—and for the most part intuitively—undergirding this pastoral practice, was gradually developed in a more systematic way. It differed from many previous theological breakthroughs in the history of the tradition inasmuch as its central development was methodological rather than thematic. It sought to theologize from a given standpoint: that of the poor. Initially at least, its concern was less with the content of theology than with its concrete rootedness. It focused less on the details of any given theological treatise than on the practical and ethical options represented there.

Such an approach, for all its penetrating intuition and moral passion, inevitably raises the question of method. This present book has as its limited and modest aim an evaluation of the fundamental assumption of this theological method. For the fundamental assumption here is that the acquisition of the perspective of the poor and an involvement in the struggle of the oppressed furnishes theology with a privileged hermeneutical perspective from which to interpret the meaning and exigencies of Christian faith. What is envisioned here, therefore, is a contribution to the contemporary debate on method in Catholic fundamental theology. Its particular area of interest is the question of hermeneutical perspective in theology. The question it specifically tackles is how and in what way a particular hermeneutical perspective—in this case the one afforded by a preferential option for the poor—can be said to provide a methodological privilege. I suggest that it does so through exercising a therapeutic function in its theological conversations with other hermeneutical perspectives. This, I will argue, consists essentially in its creating conditions for other theological perspectives to discover their rootedness in and relatedness to structures of oppression, leading to a new methodological self-awareness for theology in general.

These pages speak of an option for the poor. While the concept of "the poor" can, under certain circumstances, be legitimately spiritualized and universalized—for we are all poor before the beneficence of God—we use the term in its concrete and real sense. By it we mean, primarily and constitutively, those who want, those who are oppressed, crushed, and voiceless, those forced onto the very margins of subsistence. The religious meaning of the term can, at most, be a legitimate superimposition of meaning upon this, but it can never be a substitution. Since the contemporary globalization of poverty expands as a consequence of structures of injustice and oppression, a structural analysis is an essential, even though not exhaustive, interpretative key to exploring the issues involved.

In speaking of an option for the poor the question arises as to who makes this option. All do—or at least all are called to do so—though not all in the same way. A preliminary step to seeing the modalities of this option is to recognize—as J. B. Metz has done in such a devastating way—how bourgeois the Church has become, at least in its mentality and its language, in its formation programs, in the values behind its decision making, and in many other ways. Perhaps, at a more basic level, one needs to ask oneself how it is that the part of our planet ostensibly most

Christian is precisely the part that most blatantly exploits the rest of humankind.

Whatever their origins, in most parts of the Church those who aspire to any kind of leadership role are obliged to assume middle-class identity and values to continue to exercise such a role. Imperceptibly, they take on a value system that justifies the privatization of property, spirituality, Church, and God and thereby falsifies the biblical revelation. In this context, the option for the poor means giving priority to the standpoint and experience of the poor over their own. It means entering into a genuine dialogue and *koinōnia* with the excluded and voiceless and rereading the process and the content of revelation from this perspective. Those who are actually rich and powerful seem called to an even more profound conversion. Their dialogue with the oppressed will be for themselves a process of liberation from the tyranny of possessions and possessiveness. Apologists for a facile universalism in the Church often point to Jesus' encounter with Zacchaeus. Their argument rarely runs to prescribing the latter's subsequent behavior as a criterion for conversion, with its implicit recognition that great wealth is inevitably linked to injustice.

The poor too are called to make an option for themselves. This is essentially a willingness to engage in a dialogue that will empower them to value and trust their own experience and to see it as the very context of God's self-communication. But there are several prerequisites for this, for before they can listen with appreciation to themselves and to their own stories—something that has been and continues to be denied them—they must have the experience of being listened to. At a theological level, this demands a retrieval of the very heart of the gospel: that it really is *good news* for the poor and must not be allowed to degenerate into mere consolation or moral exhortation, much less disguised social control. For the poor too, a willingness to embark on this process involves conversion. At a profound level, it implies a readiness to be surprised by the joy of knowing that they are God's chosen ones but then, the reponsibility of living on this basis. In an ongoing way, it means liberating themselves from the patterns of immediate gratification, apathy, and a predisposition to blame and complain rather than to analyze and act, so powerfully expressed throughout the Book of Exodus and so painfully experienced wherever communities of poor people struggle to take their life and their faith into their own hands. It further extends to a preferential concern for the more hurt and exploited among themselves.

From what we are saying, it is clear that the option for the poor involves a particular kind of dialogue between what one might loosely term "middle-class intellectuals" and the poor themselves. The poor possess the raw material of suffering and oppression, which yearns for the transformation of the structures of injustice and mediates the coming of the reign of God. But part of their poverty is the internalization of these structures of oppression, depriving them for the most part of any significant degree of differentiated consciousness or analytical skill in relation to their poverty and its causes. Adequately formed theologians possess such skills—or at least comparable ones—in abundance, but the sentient base of their operations is rarely the reality of the oppressed. The process of conversion and liberation is mutual. For the theologian this demands what P. Freire has termed a "conversion to the people." If the people are to be reborn, then so also must the theologian. In seeking to root this renewed process of theologizing in the poor themselves, the reader will see that we are closer to the position of Gutiérrez than to that of Segundo. This does not explain away the difficulty of the project: it is fraught with failure and disappointment and involves a thousand beginnings. Even the theology of liberation stands under the sign of the cross!

In concrete terms, an option for the poor means the choice to attempt to love all in and through a partisan love for the oppressed. This option is a practical, existential reality, a way of living that codetermines one's manner of perceiving and understanding. For the theologian engaged in an intellectual service to the faith, it indicates not just an additional store of knowledge—though it may include this—but an adjustment of interpretative horizon through a possibly profound change in the existential reality that he or she is. We see this option as a matrix of four mutually interpenetrating dimensions comprising personal evangelical simplicity, existential solidarity with poor people, the employment of transformational socioanalytical models, and a self-critical presence in his or her own institutional context. We will develop these ideas in chapter 5.

This book, however, investigates the option for the poor not simply as an evangelical exigency but specifically as a hermeneutical perspective in theology. By "perspective" we mean the practical rootedness that codetermines the manner in which an object is viewed, perceived, and construed in one's way of thinking. Perspective is therefore more than a merely formal determination of thinking, for it also refers to qualitative elements in the structure of thought. In rather simpler terms, the way one thinks is inseparable from what one thinks, and the standpoint of one's thought is inseparable from the way one thinks and so enters the very content of thought. We see the adoption of the perspective of the option for the poor creating conditions for what H.-G. Gadamer might call a "fusion of horizons" between the immediate, though usually less differentiated, consciousness of God's privileged ones and that objectified grasp of the tradition characteristic of the theologian. In the fusion of horizons that follows on a genuinely dialogical commitment of the theologian to the poor, something new comes to be that both allows the gospel to disclose itself as good news to the poor and facilitates a qualitative step forward in the methodological self-appropriation of the tradition.

At the initial stage in the development of a liberation theology from the optic of the poor, theologians spoke of embarking on an entirely "new" theology. They insisted that it was not another "genitive theology" in the sense of applying an already established theology to either the phenomenon or the supposed concept of liberation. Instead, they sought to make liberation the horizon of theologizing. In time, they came to see that a rootedness in the praxis of liberation notwithstanding, a strictly theological enterprise demanded a theologically articulated horizon of interpretation and therefore a theological interpretation of both liberation and the option for the poor. This does not take from the primacy of praxis; it simply safeguards theological theory's inner moment within praxis. An alleged antithesis between tradition and methodological innovation gives way to a fuller understanding of theological hermeneutics.

Consequently, a naive claim to an absolute methodological privilege is replaced by a claim to a relative privilege within the ongoing theological conversation. Our task, then, is to contribute to examining and more closely defining the nature and parameters of this relative normative status. The present work seeks to make a modest original contribution in this regard. It seeks to move the debate forward by attempting to specify precisely and to what extent and within what limits the option for the poor provides theology with a privileged hermeneutical perspective.

In attempting this task, it will begin by expounding in some detail how this methodological principle is operative in the principal works of five outstanding contemporary theologians: G. Gutiérrez, J. B. Metz, L. Boff (ch. 1), J. L. Segundo, and J. Sobrino (ch. 2). Obviously, we are not embarking on a detailed study of these authors as such but rather an examination of the main methodological principle of which they are outstanding exponents. Four of these authors write from Latin America, and this reflects the origins of the theological method under consideration. Gutiérrez is the doyen of liberation theology; Boff is from the Portuguese-speaking tradition; Sobrino writes from Central America; and Segundo is essentially a methodologist. In this way a wide spread of opinion is attempted. Metz is European; he is included for a number of reasons: The emerging theology had deeper intellectual roots in European theology than it cared to acknowledge early on, and in turn, it has contributed to the methodological reorientation of First World theology. More importantly for the present discussion, the methodology under consideration is not seen as just a local theology. As explored in this book, it is considered to be a quasi-universal methodological principle.

Having elaborated how this perspective is operative in the work of our five theologians, we will then compare how each of them understands its methodological privilege. This will allow us to pose the basic question: What is its relative normative status and how can this be demonstrated? The study will then proceed to illustrate the scope, limitations, strengths, and weaknesses of this hermeneutical principle by considering five fundamental critiques of its principal methodological assumptions (chs. 3 and 4). Having clarified more exactly what we ourselves understand the option for the poor to mean in the case of the theologian (ch. 5), we will then proceed to secure the methodological foundations of this hermeneutical perspective so as to demonstrate that it is a valid, coherent, and necessary theological perspective (chs. 6 and 7). Next, we will indicate its prima facie normative status by returning to the biblical and Christological roots of theological method (ch. 8). Then, by clarifying our own position in the contemporary discussion on hermeneutics as illustrated by the Gadamer-Habermas debate (ch. 9) and applying this to theological method (ch. 10), we will seek to argue how and to what extent it is a privileged hermeneutical perspective in theology.

Abbreviations

AAS	*Acta Apostolicae Sedis*
CC	*Cross Currents*
CDF	Congregation for the Doctrine of the Faith
CELAM	Conferencia Episcopal de Latino-America
Con	*Concilium*
Greg	*Gregorianum*
ITQ	*Irish Theological Quarterly*
NB	*New Blackfriars*
NRT	*Nouvelle Revue Théologique*
OR	*Osservatore Romano*
REB	*Revista Ecclesiastica Brasileira*
RfR	*Review for Religious*
RSPT	*Revue des Sciences Philosophiques et Théologiques*
SPnC	Secretarius pro non-Credentibus
ST	*Summa theologiae*
TS	*Theological Studies*
ZfM	*Zeitschrift fuer Mission*

1

Laying the Foundations

J. B. Metz: Toward a Political Theology

Although Metz's earlier work[1] does not deal explicitly with a theological method elaborated from the optic of the poor, it does represent a decisive breakthrough in Catholic theology that provides part of the theoretical infrastructure of the theological movement under discussion. Despite an initial tendency to distance themselves from European political theology, our Latin American authors have come to accept their indebtedness. Indeed, the case for the European roots of many of their ideas has been strongly argued[2] despite the differences in tendency and method—notably concerning the importance of insertion in praxis—that remain between political and liberation theologies. For these reasons as well as for the developments in Metz's own thought, it is important to include him in this study of the hermeneutical privilege of the poor.

Metz proposed a new political theology that aimed to be a critical corrective to the privatizing tendency of much contemporary theology. Such a critical corrective would involve facing the question of the ideological superstructures in theological usage as well as the sociopolitical implications of ideas and concepts. Thus, in a phrase that was to become famous, "the deprivatization of theology is the primary critical task of political theology."

His approach was rooted in a positive acceptance of secularization, which he saw as arising fundamentally, not against Christianity but through it. Allied to a revindication of eschatology that renders impossible the privatization of the promises of the biblical tradition, his political theology sought to make contemporary theologians aware that a trial is impending between the eschatological message of Jesus and the present sociopolitical reality. Another famous theologumenon of Metz's was "the eschatological proviso," according to which every historical state of society was merely provisional, making satisfaction with the present condition of society impossible.

Living under the same "proviso," the Church can cease to exist for itself and, as the institution of the critical liberty of faith, can become the critical consciousness of society. At this stage, Metz seemed to see this primarily in terms of protecting the individual from becoming a mere cog in a completely technological future. The sociocritical dynamism of this revolutionary love would, given social injustice, have a revolutionary character in favor of freedom and justice for the sake of "the least of our brothers."

The notion of theology as critical consciousness, which overcomes the North Atlantic tendency for theology to function as a legitimation mechanism for the bourgeois subject and, consequently, articulates itself in function of a praxis of solidarity with the suffering, is significantly developed in Metz's subsequent major work, *Faith in History and in Society.*[3] This is a more systematic and detailed attempt to lay the groundwork for a "practical fundamental theology" by exposing contemporary—European—theological models as theologies of the bourgeois subject. It seeks to base a theology of all people as subjects on a retrieval of the categories of memory, narrative, and solidarity. The constant underlying reference is to the suffering, the defeated, and the unvindicated dead. In this manner he shows that he has taken seriously the criticisms of the liberation theologians, as typified by Gutiérrez, that his theology cannot penetrate the situation of dependency, injustice, and exploitation to which most of humankind is condemned.

Metz is checking theology against its ability to take the Enlightenment seriously and then to deal with it critically. This means seeing the questions posed for theology as those of the bourgeoisie and their particular privatized relationship to religion and faith. For Metz, the breakthrough of the *nouvelle théólogie* took place almost entirely within a debate with the Kant of transcendental method, the precursor of idealism. Progressive theology did not face the Kant of the philosophy of history and practical reason.

It has unconsciously enthroned the bourgeois subject. Believing itself bound to uncritically defend the latter as a religious subject, theology intensifies privatization, the instrumentalization of reason, and the devaluing of nonmarketable values such as thankfulness and the ability to mourn the suffering and the dead.

Our author sets his face against a form of evolutionary thinking that amounts to an uncritical belief in progress, conditions and shapes the contemporary person for a culture of mass apathy, and results in the emergence of a new elite equating truth with competence and evolving a praxis of control. He demonstrates, in short, how behind the dominant vision of an allegedly emancipated world lie the structures of bourgeois society and how religion has become similarily structured.

But he is not at all simplistic. Political theology can be valid only if it is theologically valid. His theology is directly opposed to a nondialectical subordination of theory to praxis.[4] Praxis remains ethically determined, but it will privilege memory as subversion and take seriously the "pathic" structure of existence. By stressing the practical nature of the Christian understanding of God in Christ,[5] Metz argues for a primacy of praxis "on the other side of idealism," taking seriously the Marxist clarification that individual moral praxis is neither socially neutral nor morally innocent. Transcendental theology—his constant conversation partner—is, by contrast, bereft of a consideration of the "conflictual contradictions and antagonistic structures of human suffering."[6] Metz points to a development in his own thought here, moving from merely critiquing existing theology to proposing a concrete option. In this light he presents his essential thesis: "The faith of Christians is a praxis in history and society that is to be understood as hope in solidarity in the God of Jesus as a God of the living and the dead who calls all people to be subjects in his presence. Christians justify themselves in this essentially apocalyptic praxis in their historical struggle for their fellow humans."[7]

Crucial to this project is the retrieval of an apocalyptically directed eschatology overcoming individualism and pointing to universal justice. The clear development here is the repeated emphasis on apocalyptic as a corrective to the contemporary evolutionary myth of time, whose openness to infinity necessarily replaces hope and fulfillment with fatalism. Apocalyptic allows us to grasp the catastrophic nature of time and thus enables the theologian to face up to the question of the world's suffering. Without it, his science degenerates into an institutionally protected timeless reflection.

Metz's proposed theology will articulate itself through the categories of memory, narrative, and solidarity. Memory includes and even privileges the memory of the suffering and the defeated and opposes a praxis of nature control based on a technocratic ideal of society whose reading of history is the history of domination. A narrative structure, no mere ornament to a "pure" concept, opposes a cybernetic use of memory that remembers only the "facts" of significance to the successful and objectifies history in function of the "story" of the victors. Drawing on Adorno's assertion that reason closed to narrative exhausts itself in reconstructions and degenerates into technique, Metz insists that narrative is not merely precritical and, thus, that theology is biographical. The believing community is a narrating community. Solidarity means the solidarity of all. When it extends to the defeated and to those who cannot survive in a society based on exchange value, it calls that society into question.

In outlining the interdependence of these three elements, Metz assigns a clear priority to the optic of the poor. His argument is that the option for the primacy of solidarity with those in need over solidarity with the "men of reason" breaks through the simulation of the equal status of partners in theological conversation. Privileging solidarity with the suffering means abandoning argumentative competence as the sole criterion for participation. This brings Metz into the very heart of the present discussion, which seeks to establish whether and in what sense a particular hermeneutical perspective—solidarity with the poor—can be assigned a methodological privilege. This "theological enlightenment of the Enlightenment" is spelled out in two other works, the first on religious life, *Followers of Christ;*[8] the second an appeal for a postbourgeois Church, *The Emergent Church.*[9] These works represent applications of his "practical fundamental theology" rather than developments in his method.

Deploring the lack of a praxis element in European Christology, he insists that the following of Christ has both a mystical and a sociopolitical element. Religion can recuperate this dual aspect of discipleship through a rediscovery of poverty's double mystical and political composition: a protest against the tyranny of possessions impelling the Christian into practical solidarity with the deprived.

The evangelical counsels must be rediscovered through transcending the inverted values of a culture based on market value. But the gap between theory and praxis suggests the danger of self-deception. His reference to Kierkegaard merits repetition: "A handsome court preacher, the cultured public's chosen one, steps forward in the magnificent castle church, faces a group of distinguished and cultured people and preaches movingly on the apostle's words: God 'chose the lowly and the despised'—And no one laughs!"[10]

In the wider ecclesiological context, Metz is asking for what he terms "a second reformation." His underlying conviction is that the Christianity of discipleship is opposed to a superstructural Christianity in the style of bourgeois religion, where the gospel risks being perverted into an endorsement of the values of those who own property. The Church must resist the temptation to take refuge in a purely interiorized spirituality and a non-threatening doctrine of love that forgets that "the universality of this love does not consist in a refusal to take sides but rather in the way it takes sides, i.e., without hatred or hostility towards people even to the foolishness of the cross."[11]

His proposed second reformation, which for Protestants will be an evocation of "grace in the senses," liberating a graceless form of humanity from its orientation to property, will be a call to freedom for Catholics—but freedom for solidarity. It will come from the periphery: neither from Rome nor from Wittenberg but "out of the liberation Christianity of the poor Churches." Its historical subject will be the poor in the poor Churches, binding together mysticism and politics and assimilating in their Eucharist social conflict and suffering. Catholics in Europe are "legasthenics in the school of bourgeois enlightenment and progress." Learning from the Base Communities of the Third World can free Catholicism from the tragedy of opening itself up to historical developments that have passed their zenith.

G. Gutiérrez-Merino: Toward a Liberation Theology

Gutiérrez's seminal work, *A Theology of Liberation,* is a basic text for any discussion of theological method from the perspective of the poor. Treating liberation as a single salvific process, Gutiérrez seeks to define theology as a critical reflection on the praxis of liberation, thus distinguishing it from traditional wisdom theology as well as from theology as the rational knowledge of the faith. Instead it "would be a critical theology worked out in the light of the word, accepted in faith and inspired by a practical purpose—and therefore indissolubly linked to historical praxis."[12] Grounded first in praxis, theology will be a second movement. The theologian will be a new kind of "organic intellectual," establishing links between the Christian understanding of salvation and the process of liberation. "Participation in the process of liberation is an obligatory and privileged locus for Christian life and reflection. In this participation will be heard nuances of the Word of God which are imperceptible in other existential situations and without which there can be no authentic and fruitful faithfulness to the Lord."[13]

Gutiérrez does not claim that this is the one and only theology but holds that it presupposes and needs the traditional models, though it will in time redefine them.

Underneath these methodological proposals lies a political vision. Liberation leaves developmentalism behind: it reads social reality in terms of dependency theory. It requires structural and class analysis and leans towards socialism. Following the "conscientization" approach of Freire, Gutiérrez stresses the participation of the poor themselves in this process. Theology will change because the Church will change. By casting its lot with those who suffer and taking their side in a partisan way, the Church will prophetically denounce institutionalized injustice, leading to simplicity of life-style and an organization free from intrigue.

Such a theology will need to develop a spirituality for conflict. The emergent theological language will have a new relationship to the social sciences. The aim of such a theology is a more efficacious commitment to liberation. With the Exodus as paradigm, interpreted with the political dimension as constitutive of the religious revelation, a lucid reflection on the theme of salvation within a single "Christo-finalized" history allows three levels of meaning of "liberation" to emerge. These are political liberation, the liberation of the human person through history, and liberation from sin for communion with God. Salvation is seen as the consummation of history, though within history and creative of history. Going beyond an individualistic morality, Gutiérrez's emphasis on history unmasks spiritualizing processes and, similar to Metz, though without reference to him, emphasizes the denunciative aspects of eschatology.

A spirituality of liberation centers on a conversion to the oppressed person and the exploited social class. It means participating in their struggle. Gutiérrez suggests that theology has not yet produced the categories necessary to express that option. Moreover, purely "theological" categories would not be enough. What is required is "a vital attitude, all-embracing and synthesizing," allowing us to break with familiar mental categories. Gutiérrez is himself a striking example of the process he is arguing here:[14] he is not just theorizing.

In elaborating the relationship between politics and eschatology, he links up with Bloch's retrieval of Utopian thinking, stressing its rational nature, its relation to historical reality, and its verification through praxis, linking these with the three levels of liberation. His point is that the space of Utopia can provide the context for a fruitful point of contact between faith and politics. With Freire, he affirms that in a situation of oppression only the oppressed can work out Utopias that are not reformist ideologies.

Gutiérrez applies these theological principles to the Church, not hesitating to describe the situation as one of institutional moral failure on the verge of bankruptcy. The first step is to recognize that a partisan stand has already been taken and that a pretense of noninvolvement in politics is a subterfuge for conservatism. Arguing that class struggle is an undeniable fact,[15] he points out the contradiction of interclassist doctrine and calls again for a partisan love for the poor that privileges the oppressed. The universality of Christian love can be arrived at only through particularity. This, in turn, calls for a new and dialectical understanding of the unity of the Church.

In his later works, especially *The Power of the Poor in History,* Gutiérrez elaborates these basic ideas. In relation to the question of theological method, there is some sharpening of focus. However, a certain development in nuance is still lacking, as in the following manner of expressing the primacy of praxis: "Nevertheless the relationship between deed and word is asymmetric—what basically counts is the deed. Of course it will not do to overemphasize this or push it to extremes. . . . Only in this unity of deed and word is there any sense of the distinctions we make."[16]

Liberation theology represents the right of the poor to think, and the methodological quantum leap it requires will only be possible when the exploited, as artisans of their own liberation, can theologize for themselves. Gutiérrez's own involvement in this process has effected changes in his use of language, resulting in what could be termed "inaccuracies" or "oversimplifications," as in the above quotation. Here he seems insufficiently nuanced in actually spelling out the implications of the reflexive relation between word and deed.

For the Church—in Latin America—to "recover the memory of the scourged Christ of the Indies"[17] demands profound conversion. In short, it means breaking its ties with the present order. Theology must discover the poor person as the revealer of the "utterly other." By seeing that poor person in his or her social class, it will accept the present moment with its historical contradictions as a *locus theologicus*. Theology will then be a critical reflection from within an option for this social class. "Hence the theologian must be personally involved in the liberation process. Such involvement is necessary not only for concrete results, but for genuinely scientific work as well."[18]

There would appear to be a development here in that liberative praxis is seen not merely as an evangelical exigency but equally as a condition for scientific rigor. Regrettably, Gutiérrez does not elaborate on this point. Still, he will not allow his method to be disqualified from theological reflection: to refuse to believe that the poor can do theology is to deny them the right to think. Theology is always elaborated out of praxis: consciously or not, the theologian always has a given point of departure.

For liberation theology, the interlocutor is the one who becomes a nonperson through oppression, and thus this theology is in historical contradiction with the "progressive theology" of the modern bourgeois spirit. Rootedness in the poor does not render it less scientific. "Rather it would seem that the scientific rigor and rationality of a concrete theology is something so unfamiliar to the system's dominators, and to those who depend on the ideology of the dominators, that it seems to them to lack rigor and reason. In any case, it is certainly a fact that direct participation in a concrete historical process in the struggles of the poor and in popular expressions of the faith, affords a perception of aspects of the Christian message that escapes other approaches."[19]

Whatever distancing from European theology that was evident in earlier works is left behind in a splendid exegesis of the famous letter of Bonhoeffer to Eberhard Bethge of 8 June 1944. Gutiérrez does not attempt to argue his own position from Bonhoeffer: "The protest movements of the poor or the contemporary labor movement find no place in Bonhoeffer's historical focus." The point of connectedness derives from the latter's famous thesis on God's weakness. The only God is the God who saves us not through his domination but through his suffering, allowing Bonhoeffer to conclude that it is not the religious act that makes the Christian but the participation in the sufferings of God in the secular life. Gutiérrez finds it unwarranted to deduce from this that we are in the presence of a critical analysis of modern society on the grounds of that society's injustice. But Bonhoeffer and Gutiérrez join each other in privileging a theological method that takes its point of departure in reading history from below.[20]

Gutiérrez's long-standing suggestion that a theology from the perspective of the poor requires a new spirituality finds expression in his next major work, *We Drink from Our Own Wells*.[21] Here we see in action a theology from the perspective of the poor articulating a spirituality. There is no explicit treatment of theological method, though his remarks on conversion and role reversal implicitly point to two methodological aspects: the pretheological rootedness of theology and the methodological condition of learning from the oppressed.

Arguing that every great spirituality is tied to the great historical movements of its epoch, Gutiérrez concludes that the irruption of the poor into the struggle for profound social change represents such a movement, retracing the scriptural meaning of the journey of the people in search of God. Participation involves an inversion of roles. Those formed in the "schools of spirituality" must become learners from the experience of the poor.

Entry into the experience of the poor, however, does not mean renouncing the rich traditions of the history of spirituality but rather employing them to enrich the actual lived spirituality of the poor. Equally, Gutiérrez stresses that an interpretation of the liberationist perspective that leaves out personal conversion is a caricature. Nor is his proposal a form of activism: The struggle for historical efficacy takes place within the gratuitousness of grace.

Journeying with the poor through the *noche obscura* of injustice can be frightening, demanding a new form of spiritual childhood. For perhaps the first time in his writings, Gutiérrez allows himself to speak of the power of personal sin that is among the poor themselves. Their world, too, is "pervaded with the force of life and death, of grace and sin. In that world we find indifference . . . individualism . . . hearts closed to the Lord. Insofar as the poor are part of human history, they are not free of the motivations found in the two cities of which Augustine spoke: love of God and love of self." Being realistic about the titanic task involved means that "it will be necessary therefore to undertake the commitment knowing in advance that the situation of the poor will almost certainly overstrain the human capacity for solidarity."[22]

Here there will be a profound and powerful solitude calling for a new solidarity. For the desert can be crossed only in community.

L. Boff: A Theology of Captivity and Liberation

At first glance, Boff's initial work on the methodology of a new theology, *Teologia do Cativeiro e da Libertação*,[23] closely mirrors Gutiérrez's *Theology of Liberation*. There is the same emphasis on liberation as opposed to dependency; the need for thinking in structural terms and surpassing privatized morality; the primacy of praxis; the shortcomings of European theology, including political theology; and the need for political choices in favor of the poor as well as the ecclesiological implications, seen, like Gutiérrez, in terms of the inexhaustible subversive meaning of the Exodus. One of the differences is Boff's emphasis on the nature control endemic to Western thinking, which, at this stage of his reflections, he saw as the primary generator of oppression through the capitalist system, which is a product of this process.

He also extends the theological problematic of injustice and oppression to ask how theology can articulate reconciliation with past oppressors and have solidarity with the dead and wounded of all sides. The dominant ideology writes history as the history of conquerors, repressing dialectical reason in favor of a technical instrumentalization of reason that never thematizes human suffering. The history of Brazil, to cite his own example, *"foi escrita pela mão branca."*[24]

For Boff, before the question of the methodological character of theology arises there is first the irruption of the appalling reality of poverty into one's consciousness. Discovering the "other of the oppressed" allows an intuitive though not yet critically articulated faith-grasp of the situation. It needs a socioanalytical model.

Thus the theology under discussion is not just another genitive theology. Acquiring the standpoint of the humiliated needs not only adequate theoretical mediation but also more fundamentally transformational praxis, for without this there will only be the vocabulary of the option for the poor. Yet when it comes to the place of the theologian in this praxis, Boff, at this stage of the development of his thought, seems less thoroughgoing than Gutiérrez. "All this does not necessarily imply that the theologian leaves his chair and goes and inserts himself among the popular classes. He can live a committed life on the basis of his theoretic commitment exercised within a profound and clear option for the oppressed. His function is that of an organic intellectual. Contact with the base is enriching, maintaining vigilance on his language. . . . His destiny is at another level of the struggle."[25]

Boff elaborates what is essentially a theological reworking of Freire in proposing the process of liberation of the oppressed as the means of the evangelization of the oppressor. To speak significantly of the liberation of Christ in a situation of oppression means that our questions are oriented by a clear interest. Boff seems to choose a critical social analysis to express this interest on the grounds that it is the one demanded by the exigencies of the present time. There is always an optic from which we read the words and historical actions of Jesus. Today, Boff argues, we are simply making conscious an inevitable hermeneutical procedure. A merely descriptive reading of the liberative praxis of Jesus would leave its significance in the past tense.

Here Boff is resuming, though with some development, his earlier Christological reflections.[26] There he presented Jesus as privileging the marginalized, who are nearer the kingdom than all others and who follow Jesus because from an established order that cannot redeem their alienation, they have nothing to gain.

As a preliminary step to thinking Christologically in this vein, Boff asserted the hermeneutical primacy of the anthropological over the ecclesiastical, of the Utopian over the merely factual, of the critical over the dogmatic, of the social over the individual, and of orthopraxis over orthodoxy. With this optic, his approach would seek to go beyond a typical historical-critical investigation into the origins of Christological titles and attempt to see the meaning of the person of Jesus being disclosed in his identification with the marginalized.

A reflection on the specific contribution of the Church to liberation[27] located the problematic within a view of dependency generated by the transnational imperialism of capitalism as the dominant cause of oppression. The role of the Christian community is not reducible to the moral condemnation of the capitalist system but is a matter of overcoming it concretely and historically. The basic question seems to have become political. The theological basis for the option for the poor is that the poor possess a sacramental function; in them we meet the Lord in a privileged way. Consequently, the question of the specific function of the Church can only be answered in terms of a fundamental option for the poor.

With specific reference to religious, Boff suggests that the option for the poor can be concretized in three ways: to live for the poor by assuming their cause and their optic; by changing one's social position and participating directly in the conscientizing and liberating process; and by living as one of the poor, sharing the burden of oppression.[28] In a later development of these ideas he seeks to root spirituality in general in a retrieval of what he terms "essential poverty." By this he means the ontological-created status of the person before God. It is, he argues, the devaluation of this that created the tendencies that are concretized in the structures of oppression.[29] He does not refer specifically to the theologian in this division, nor does he discuss how each of the levels might interpenetrate the others.

Some of the hermeneutical aspects of a theology articulated from the optic of the poor are evident in Boff's ecclesiology. He does not make an exclusivist claim for this theology, admitting that no tendency can claim a monopoly and each must recognize its limitations.[30] With a certain degree of pragmatism, he suggests that the determining factor is whichever theology is necessary here and now. In outlining the parameters of a contemporary theological method, he implies some development in his methodology.

> After Marx, theology could no longer put into parenthesis the material conditions of life without the charge of mystifying the reality of iniquitous conditions. The theological word concerning the social realm has credibility only as second word, i.e., after having done justice to the above situations. Against both theoretical pragmatism and epistemological idealism, one must recognize that the practice of theology implies two separate and distinct areas: internal and external. The first is defined by the authority of theory where rules must be respected. The second corresponds to theology's dependence on the social conditions of production or the economy of social goods, over which the theologian is called to exercise a constant ideo-political watch.[31]

The distinction between the internal and external areas of theology also figures in the epilogue to his Christology.[32] Commitment of itself will not guarantee the intrinsic quality of a theology.

This ecclesiological critique argues that the exercise of power and the various processes in the Church can only be understood by viewing the Church as it is socially organized in the world. Sensing an ecclesiastical analogy to the worldly expropriation of the means of production, Boff fears that the religious-ecclesiastical realm has also been adjusted to the interests of its ruling class. As with ideology in society, theology can here too be allowed a solely legitimating function.

He sees the way forward through the Base Communities, understood as a new way of being Church: namely, the confrontation of social contradictions by believing communities of poor people in the light of the gospel. The option for the poor repeats the divine option; the rights of the poor are the rights of God. This option is for the poor and against their poverty. It involves moving from an elitist position of working for the poor to mobilizing their "historic power" in becoming a Church of the poor. He explains what he means by terming it a "preferential" option.

> Preferential is not a synonym for "more" or "special." The meaning here is more radical and is apparent when one analyzes the causes which generate social poverty. The poor per-

> son does not stand alone: he stands in relation to the rich person
> who exploits him and with his allies from the other classes who
> support him in his struggle. Therefore to opt preferentially for
> the poor means: to love the poor first, as Jesus did, then start-
> ing from the poor to love all others, inviting them to liberate
> themselves from the mechanisms of the production of riches
> on the one hand and poverty on the other. . . . The Church
> loves the poor inasmuch as she combats, not rich persons, but
> the socio-economic mechanisms which make them rich at the
> cost of the poor.[33]

Thus, the option is not an exclusive sectarianism but a way of expressing the Catholicity of the faith. Boff repeats the criticism, common to all the authors under discussion in this chapter, that even *Gaudium et spes,* while acknowledging inequality and denouncing it, did not examine its structural causes. A theology from the perspective of the poor in the form of liberation theology is, he argues, a creative reception of Vatican II. His argument is based on Congar's notion of *réception,*[34] which argues the right of the people of God not just to receive a truth, but to elaborate it within a contemporary codification; the destinaries of a text become its coauthors. Thus, liberation theology is the social teaching of the Church elaborating itself within the socio-historical reality of the "Third World," and the "original meaning" acquires new resonances in a different situation.[35]

Notes

[1] J. B. Metz, *Zur Theologie der Welt* (Mainz, 1968); English trans., *Theology of the World* (London, 1970). This represents Metz's thought from 1961 to 1967 and is an attempt to focus on questions Vatican II "despite its admirable progress did not consider" (p. 8).

[2] J. Moltmann, "An Open Letter to J. M. Bonino" in (eds.) G. H. Anderson and T. F. Stransky, *Mission Trends,* vol. 4, *Liberation Theologies* (New York and Grand Rapids, 1979) 57–70. On p. 64 Moltmann states, "The conclusion that 'orthopraxis rather than orthodoxy becomes the criterion for theology' is a literal quote from Metz." First published in *Christianity and Crisis,* March 29, 1976.

[3] J. B. Metz, *Glaube in Geschichte und Gesellschaft* (Mainz, 1977); English trans., *Faith in History and Society* (London, 1980). This work is a synthesis of a reworking of a series of previously published articles. Much the same could be said of several of the works to be examined in this chapter, including several by Boff and, notably, Gutiérrez's *Power of the Poor in History.* A minute examination of the layers of development is outside the scope of the present work. One can see the contributions to theological method in the final editions.

⁴The relation between theory and praxis will be discussed in ch. 7. Metz's reflexive relation between theory and praxis distinguishes him from some of his followers in the *Kritischer Katholicismus* school—as it does the other authors being discussed in chs. 1 and 2.

⁵Metz demands "dass Christus immer so gedacht werden muss, dass er nie nur gedacht ist," *Glaube in Geschichte und Gesellschaft*, 48.

⁶There are more references to K. Rahner in this book than to any other author. Metz continually expresses his indebtedness to and admiration for his former professor, but at this stage he has moved beyond his position, even rejecting it, as he does in ch. 9 of this work. In an interview in his latter years (Freiburg, 1984), Rahner expressed hurt at some of Metz's remarks. Ironically, Gutiérrez had earlier made a virtually identical criticism of Metz! Cf. *Faith in History and in Society*, 45.

⁷Ibid., 73.

⁸*Zeit der Orden: Zur Mystik und Politik der Nachfolge* (Freiburg, 1977); English trans., *Followers of Christ* (London, 1978).

⁹*Jenseits Bürgerlicher Religion: Reden ueber die Zukunft des Christentums* (Mainz, 1980); English trans., *The Emergent Church* (London, 1982). With the exception of the article "The Faith of the Reformers" (1968), this book is an anthology of Metz's principal articles from 1978 to 1980.

¹⁰S. Kierkegaard, *Journals and Papers* (London, 1967f.) 3:594, cited by Metz in *Followers of Christ*, 58.

¹¹*The Emergent Church*, 4.

¹²*Teología de la Liberación: Perspectivas* (Lima, 1971); English trans., *A Theology of Liberation* (New York, 1973) 4–5. *See also* "Notes for a Theology of Liberation," TS 31:2 (1970) 243–261.

Gutiérrez first wrote in this vein in *La Pastoral de la Iglesia en America Latina* (Montivideo, 1968), cf. p. 15. Some of its principal intellectual roots are in the works of Blondel and Marx, whose eleventh thesis on Feuerbach, "Die Philosophen haben die Welt nur verschieden interpretiert, es kommt darauf an sie zu veraendern," is a virtual *Grundaxiom* for liberation theology.

¹³*A Theology of Liberation*, 49.

¹⁴Cf. R. McAfee Brown, *Gustavo Gutiérrez* (Atlanta, 1980).

¹⁵*A Theology of Liberation*, 273.

¹⁶*La Fuerza Histórica de los Pobres* (Lima, 1979); English trans., *The Power of the Poor in History* (New York, 1983). This work is essentially an anthology of articles by Gutiérrez during the previous eight years (cf. p. 17).

¹⁷This is a classic statement of Bartolomé de las Casas, "Historia de las Indias," *Obras* 2:356, as quoted by Gutiérrez (p. 194f.).

Juan Gines de Sepúlveda is presented as an apologist for the "theology" of the conquistadores; Francisco de Vitoria, as a "centrist theologian." Las Casas articulates the presence of Christ in the "scourged Indians." Gutiérrez attempts to indicate a parallel at both the political and the theological level between then and now. Cf. P.-I. André-Vincent, "Le prophétisme de Barthelemy de las Casas," NRT 101:4 (1979) 541–560, with many references to las Casas' *Obras;* also R. Marcus, "Las Casas: admirateur critique de Vitoria," Sup 160 (March 1987) 73–83. This whole issue of *Le Supplément* is devoted to the famous debates between Vitoria and las Casas.

¹⁸*The Power of the Poor in History*, 73, n. 23.

¹⁹Ibid., 192.

[20]Gutiérrez quotes with agreement what must remain the most famous and most moving statement of theology from the underside of history: "It is an experience of incomparable value to have learned to see the great events of history from beneath: from the viewpoint of the useless, the suspect, the abused, the powerless, the despised—in a word, from the viewpoint of those who suffer." D. Bonhoeffer, *Letters and Papers from Prison,* ed. E. Bethge (exp. ed. New York, 1987) 177.

[21]*Beber en su Proprio Pozo* (Lima, 1983); English trans., *We Drink from Our Own Wells* (New York, 1984) cf. p. 46.

[22]Ibid., 126.

[23]*Teologia do Cativeiro e da Libertação* (Petropolis, 1976).

[24]*Teologia do Cativeiro e da Libertação* 112. Cf. Boff, "Historia da Igreja no Brasil," REB 37:146 (1977) 368-372. Also M. V. Rezando, *Não se pode Servir a dois Senhores* (Lins, 1980).

[25]*Teologia do Cativeiro e da Libertação,* 34.

[26]*Jesus Cristo Libertador* (Petropolis, 1972), English trans., *Jesus Christ Liberator* (London, 1980). In charting developments in Boff's theological methodology, bear in mind that the epilogue published in the English edition was written in January 1978, several years later than the original work.

[27]*A Fé na Periferia do Mundo* (Petropolis, 1978) 58-61.

[28]Ibid., 75.

[29]*Vida segundo O Espiritu* (Petropolis, 1981) 114.

[30]*Igreja: Carisma e Poder* (Petropolis, 1981); English trans., *The Church: Charism and Power* (London, 1983) cf. p. 12. Boff replied to the many critics of this work in "Igreja: Carisma e Poder—uma justificação contra falsas leituras," REB 42:166 (1982) 227-260.

[31]*Do Lugar do Pobre* (Petropolis, 1984) 42.

[32]*Jesus Christ Liberator,* 272, cf. n. 26 above. Here Boff has been clearly influenced by the work of his brother Clodovis Boff, O.S.M. We discuss the latter in detail in ch. 3.

[33]*Do Lugar do Pobre,* 37.

[34]Y. Congar, "La réception comme Realité Ecclésiologique," RSPT 56 (1972) 369-403.

[35]*Do Lugar do Pobre,* 35.

2

Toward the Methodological Question

J. L. Segundo: Theology and Ideology

The earlier work of J. L. Segundo, especially the five volumes of *Theology for the Artisans of a New Humanity,* can be seen as an elaboration of his belief that the long-standing stress on individual salvation in the next world represents a distortion of Jesus' "message" and has resulted in an equally distorted pastoral practice. His aim was a mature and responsible theology, moving from a bank-deposit understanding of grace and the sacraments to conceiving and reformulating their meaning in function of a community whose liberative action is secular and historical. His ecclesiology would "analyze the temporal consequences of the errors into which the Church is drawn by the lure of power rather than the consequences of service."[1]

His departure from what might appear to be liberal preoccupations becomes clearer in his treatment of the theology of God. If the liberal debate is on "the death of God," his question is, What God? since "our falsified and inauthentic ways of dealing with our fellow men are allied to our falsifications of the idea of God. Our unjust society and our perverted idea of God are in close and terrible alliance."[2]

A new theological hermeneutics is called for, involving four decisive factors: suspicion of the dominant ideology following from the experience of oppression; an application of this suspicion to society's superstructure, including theology; a parallel exegetical suspicion following a new mode of religious experience; and a new hermeneutic.

Echoing Moltmann's contention that the goal of Christian universalism can only be won through the dialectical process of opting for the oppressed, Segundo suggests an inversion of the ordinary relation between evangelical values and social praxis, arguing that a real effective option for the oppressed can deideologize our minds and free our thinking for the gospel message. "One cannot simply have recourse to an *a priori* understanding of the Gospel since one's interpretation will be in function of prior commitments—something that can be seen in the *Redaktionsgeschichte* of the gospels themselves."[3]

The underlying assumption in much modern theology seems to be that the existing situation, that is, liberal democracy, is somehow ideology free, which, Segundo argues, is impossible, since all ideas are bound up with social situations at least in an unconscious way. Faith and ideology are inextricably mixed. Faith is the transcendent value-structure, referring to absolute values, while ideology is that which gives direction to the means to effect a nonempirically chosen value. For Segundo, faith, although not an ideology, has sense only as the foundation for ideologies. Scripture is an account of a "deuterolearning": learning how to learn with the help of ideologies. A faith without ideology is a dead faith.

Ideology will determine the choice of sociology. A pretheological commitment to change rules out a positivist-behaviorist model. This leads Segundo to consider the crucial question of the possible relation between Marxian sociology and a theology articulated from a liberative praxis in favor of the poor. In proposing this path, Segundo stresses two aspects of the question. First, Marx failed to apply to religion with adequate rigor his own theory of superstructure. For if religion is supposed to arise from the material conditions that follow from the division of labor, then it should be ambiguous rather than invalid. Second, basing himself on Engels,[4] Segundo argues that historical materialism cannot be reduced to economism. Aware that he is developing a view not shared by official Marxist sociologists, he has continued in *Faith and Ideologies*[5] to devote a lot of energy to demonstrating that historical materialism at the ideological level is not necessarily atheistic or empiricist. He does this not only on the basis of what Marx and Engels wrote but by arguing that since both atheism and empiricism involve transcendent judgments that are per se transideological, they cannot be empirically verified and thus may not be described as "scientific" in the way Marx and orthodox Marxists spoke of "science," that is, a hypothesis subject to empirical verifiability.

Because ideology is effective only in politics, every theology is a political theology. A theology that performs its political function unconsciously is always conservative. A theology on the side of the oppressed is simply conscious in its ideological analysis. A putatively impartial theology is methodologically impossible. Thus the relationship between politics and theology is decisive.

Segundo's subsequent work spells out the implications of this view of the interpenetration of faith and ideology for Christology. In *The Historical Jesus of the Synoptics*,[6] he seeks to demonstrate how fundamentally political is the message and praxis of Jesus and at the same time, by approaching the political dimension with total seriousness, to demonstrate the abiding religious significance of Jesus. He wishes to prevent Jesus from being turned into an idol, a development most likely in vaunted claims to ideological neutrality.

For Segundo, the very depoliticization of Christianity "is a far more politicized version of the Gospel than any of the denigrated political re-readings that are being made to-day."[7] Jesus is not only political, he is partisan. The kingdom he proclaims points to a clear preference for certain groups. In spelling out the political dimensions of Jesus, Segundo is at pains to demonstrate that the decisive political power was not the Romans but the internal socioreligious structure. "Viewed in societal terms, Palestine continued to be a theocracy even when it had . . . become a colony." In this light, the religious discrediting of the scribes and Pharisees "was rightly viewed as subversive political activity": "Someone who is systematically destroying the real authority of the dominant group in a theocracy—even if or rather precisely because, he is doing that in religious terms—becomes a fearful political adversary. Framed in the domestic context, the social structure of Israel, Jesus is much more markedly political with his religious message than are the Zealots in their activity."[8]

Segundo finds it "incredible that in the elaboration of Christologies, greater attention has not been paid to Jesus' systematic dismantling of oppressive religious ideology." Discipleship demands "all the clear-sightedness, heroism and commitment" of Jesus himself in this regard. Jesus is "generating an historical conflict," placing "historical causality in the service of the kingdom." This theological reading has hermeneutical implications. "There is a change in the ontological value-premises with respect to the two camps in which Israelite society is divided in Jesus' day. This should logically entail a parallel change in the epistemological premises on the basis of which divine revelation (i.e., the Law) is interpreted."[9]

The nonarrival of the kingdom leads to a change of interpretative key within the New Testament communities. This change of key is illustrated in great detail by an in-depth exegesis of most of Paul's Letter to the Romans by Segundo in his next major work, *The Humanist Christology of Paul.* Paul's process of Christological creation, employing a different literary genre, uses an anthropological rather than a political key. But Paul's anthropology will "open out into historical causality and politics by virtue of [its] own inner dynamics and fidelity to the Jesus of the Gospels."[10]

Segundo's theory of ideology is clearly in the background when he notes that Paul's Christians stop worrying about what is licit "and start asking themselves whether a given course of action is suitable or not," thus incorporating historical causality. In this way, he seeks to argue that only those projects that face up to resistance to love and overcome it "as effectively as possible will constitute a definitive service to the plan of God." Thus, although Paul, unlike Jesus, does not directly confront sociopolitical structures, his anthropological scheme clearly discloses the manner in which "religion" can marginalize human beings in the name of the deity.

In attempting to spell out the political significance of this exegesis of Paul, Segundo returns to Jesus' death considered as the consequence of a partisan and conflictive option. He insists, however, that "it makes no sense to try to prove the perduring superiority of Jesus of Nazareth in political matters." The context has changed. "To copy or mimic" what Jesus said to the poor "is idealism."

No interpretative key can itself become a dogma. Obviously, Segundo is not suggesting a Christology that does not issue in political consequences as concrete and conflictual as those of Jesus. His point is that liberation theology should avoid a restricted understanding of politics as the only valid interpretation of Christology. It must avoid the temptation to look for "an immediate pragmatic connection between the problems arising on our practical horizon and the solution offered by the life and praxis of Jesus."[11] This would be to bypass real praxis.

Segundo believes that Paul's situation is more like his than is Jesus', and so he is drawn to it "from politics." "We can proceed to re-read Paul in his spirit, not in his letters, just as he himself teaches us to do with the rest of biblical revelation." This means reading Paul in a political context because of the sociopolitical structures of sin. Paul has taught us not to equate sin with the specific sins of human weakness. "In short, Paul has helped us to see the central problem of our human condition to-day: the creation and maintenance of structures and power-centers that are bound to block all effective forms of loving our neighbors and our fellow human beings in either the public or the private sector."[12]

This insistence becomes a starting point for a critique of liberation theology's belief that Paul is apolitical. Because of not reading Paul closely, "it has created its own image of a simultaneous qualitative and quantitative power: 'the People' or more specifically 'the poor.'" For Segundo, this is an oversimplistic and mistaken eschatology, which in the long run will only intensify people's desperation and despair.

Even Gutiérrez does not escape from the criticism of attributing to the poor a power for transformation in which Segundo detects simplistic and triumphalistic elements. We find here echoes of the tendency toward elitism already present in Segundo's ecclesiology.[13] The impression is given that Segundo's Church would be composed of an enlightened minority, an elite, operating as a vanguard in the transformation of the world. It is a model that might easily invite unwelcome comparisons. This model appears to be quite different from the notion of a Church embedded in the poor themselves. Even the conscientization project is questioned as an ecclesial praxis, for the reason that the gospel is presumed to run counter to populist tendencies.

In the belief that he has found in Paul "a more ecologically sound vision of the human realm," Segundo leaves behind any quantitative approach. His is an avowedly minority Church. It seems to us that he ultimately rejects a theology rooted in a praxis where " 'the lowliest of the poor' gain their own voice," principally because, to him, it would represent an empiricist inversion of quality and quantity. To Gutiérrez's project of the gospel read from the standpoint of the poor and convoking a Church of the poor, he suggests that "from the hermeneutic side it is rather curious that Gutiérrez does not ask himself why Jesus did not succeed in his own day in getting his own people, his own poor people, to snatch God's revelation, the Law and the Prophets, from the hands of the great ones of Israel."[14]

On this reading, Segundo's theology seems to be in favor of the liberation of the poor, but it is not rooted in them and they do not contribute to articulating it.

J. Sobrino: The Struggle of the Poor as the Condition of the Possibility of Theology

Sobrino, in *Christology at the Crossroads,* develops the Christological basis of the option for the poor. In doing so, he not only provides a striking example of a theology from the perspective of the poor, but—implicitly for the most part—makes the case for the methodologically privileged status of this theological method in that it makes possible a nonidolatrous notion of God. The mystery of God is accessible only to those who draw near to the poor.

He expresses a threefold suspicion of traditional Christology on the grounds of its abstract neutrality, which eliminates the prophetic denunciative aspect, thus exempting Christians from the conflict-ridden toils of history. He argues for a Christology conscious of its presuppositions and its motivating generic interest. With Marx's eleventh thesis on Feuerbach as a hermeneutical key, he insists, following Boff, that we study Christology so that Jesus' *ipsissima intentio* may emerge to pave the way for effective collaboration with him.

Sobrino builds on what other theologians like Boff, Gutiérrez, Metz, and Segundo have said about Jesus' option for the oppressed but succeeds in giving the theme greater theological depth. He sees Jesus' praxis as a partisan option for the sake of unrestricted solidarity based not only on compassion but as the key to community. He presents Jesus as "immersing himself in the situation on the basis of a 'class outlook.' " But, aware that a retrojection of twentieth-century class analysis would be anachronistic, he clarifies his argument.

> The term "class outlook" is meant to be somewhat ambiguous because in Jesus' case its meaning is not crystal clear. Yet there are certain elements which help us to see what his understanding of justice from a "class outlook" means. First, the poor are the people who understand the meaning of the kingdom best, even though their knowledge and understanding comes by way of contrariety. Second, Jesus reinforces his experience of the necessity for justice through his contact with the poor. Third, Jesus' service to the totality is concretized directly in his service to the poor. Fourth, in his own personal life he experiences poverty. At the very least it is a relative poverty that somehow includes him in the ranks of the poor. Fifth, Jesus undergoes the experience of class identity and specifically the consequences of his fellowship with the group known as the poor. The power wielded by the other major group in society is directed against him.[15]

The following of Jesus cannot be reduced to mere imitation because an essential feature of Jesus' morality was its localization in history. Since the very principle of incarnation involves the adoption of a partial stance, Jesus can be followed only by allowing oneself and one's viewpoint to be shaped by the poor.

Drawing on Moltmann's theology of the cross,[16] Sobrino sets out to preserve its scandalous force, so often emasculated into a merely noetic mystery. Interpreting the cross as the outcome of God's primordial option, he argues that the identification of the Crucified with the estranged and marginalized makes the mystery of God accessible only to those who draw near to the poor. Since the cross is the outcome of an option, spirituality consists in following this option.

If the "otherness" of God is primordially revealed in the otherness of the oppressed, then an option for the oppressed is a prerequisite for any reflection on God; thus, the option for the poor constitutes the condition of the possibility of theology and its method.

Sobrino is less interested in justifying Christology before the "bar of reason" than before the "yearnings of a transformative praxis," even if he does not sidestep the challenge posed by the Enlightenment. He poses a fundamental question on the relative status of different theological models when he states: "The two standpoints are not mutually exclusive, of course, but the emphasis given to one or the other will shift the thrust and direction of a given Christology. . . . European theology has been more interested in demonstrating the truth of Christ before the bar of reason. . . . (We) seek to show how the truth of Christ is capable of transforming a sinful world."[17]

The same thrust is evident in Sobrino's later work, *The True Church of the Poor,* where a comparison of European and Latin American theology again privileges a concern for transformation over mere rationality. "I think therefore that in comparing different theological understandings, a detailed investigation of the methods of theological analysis is less important than an investigation of the practical and ethical options represented by the understanding."[18]

The essential thesis of the work is that the poor are the authentic ecclesiological *lugar teologico.* Here there is an important development in his thought. The poor are no longer just the recipients of the fruits of theology and the praxis it informs. They are the condition of the possibility of both. Proceeding on the basis of "God's scandalous and partisan love for the poor," he poses the priority of transformation over development as the key to the future and thence argues the primacy of dialectical over analogical reasoning in theology.

The poor are the privileged ecclesiological locus because they are the agents of conversion. "The poor are not only the privileged addressees of evangelization, they are also the condition of the possibility of evangelization inasmuch as the evangelization of the poor is constitutive of the very content."[19]

For Sobrino, something akin to a resurrection appearance is given in the grace of seeing Christ in the poor. The Church of the poor is not a Church for the poor, constructed in logical independence from the poor. The Church of the poor is not a section, not even a privileged section, of the Church. It means forming the Church on the basis of the poor as the structural principle of its organization and mission. Here Sobrino goes beyond the notion of Church as a universalistic, theologically democratic people with an ethical concern for the poor.

Sobrino's argument is that since God moves indefectibly by way of the poor, they are the authentic theological source for the understanding of Christian truth and praxis. Their situation provides the epistemological vantage point from which we can understand theologically. Conceding that the poor themselves are not theologians, he nevertheless makes the rather absolute claim that they are the ultimate source of theology's own originality.[20]

Thus Sobrino, by implication, is saying that a theology from within an option for the poor is the only valid theology because evangelization is constituted only within this option, and for him this is uniquely Christian: constitutive, one might say, of the uniqueness of Christianity. His argument, as we have seen, would go as follows: The transcendence of the one true God is revealed in the Crucified, and this true God is mediated in a privileged way by the poor. Thus the option for the poor facilitates the epistemological break necessary to draw near to God. The poor are therefore the hermeneutical instance making possible a reading of the tradition that reveals God.

The Project: A Theology from the Perspective of the Poor: Different Understandings of Its Hermeneutical Status

Metz, although initially less rooted in praxis, does lay part of the theoretical groundwork. His deprivatized theology cares for the "least of the brethren," but it is not rooted in them. This, however, is developed into an articulation of solidarity with all the oppressed and unremembered dead and includes a politicized retrieval of Christian life and the evangelical counsels.

For Gutiérrez, theology is a critical reflection on liberative praxis and therefore rooted in it, and without this rootedness will miss out on fundamental nuances of the Word. Like Metz, he sees his theology in historical contradiction with "progressive theology," and both share the project of reading history from below. Gutiérrez, in elaborating his spirituality, has demonstrated that this theological model is not reductionist.

Boff closely mirrors Gutiérrez, though he seems at times to emphasize the philosophical rather than the practical roots of his position. He has raised the question of how theology from this perspective articulates reconciliation with all, but he has not developed this to the extent that Metz has. His work has included wide applications of his theological insights. Boff's early work is less clearly differentiated from traditional theology.

Segundo, whose work ranges equally widely, has emphasized the epistemological and methodological assumptions. Rather than articulating a theology from the perspective of the poor, he assumes a theology at the service of the poor and seeks to justify some of its presuppositions.

Sobrino follows Boff in seeking to elucidate the *ipsissima intentio* of Jesus. He is more nuanced than either Gutiérrez or Boff in seeking to spell out the Christological basis of the option for the poor, and he has highlighted theology's rootedness in the experience of the poor to the extent of arguing that it cannot be constructed in logical independence from them.

The Theologian and the Project

Metz exposes the "progressive" theologian as an apologist for the bourgeois subject. The theologian must not only take the Enlightenment seriously, he or she must also deal critically with it. In arguing later that the historical subject of a new theology will be the poor of the liberation Church, Metz has rejoined, as it were, the position of Gutiérrez.

For the Peruvian, the theologian is an organic intellectual who actually participates in the liberative praxis of the poor. Theology henceforth will come more from these groups than from the traditional centers. The recognition of having already taken a partisan stand prompts a new class-based insertion in social reality. For Gutiérrez, this is a condition even for scientific work. Theology is worth doing because it contributes to this praxis of liberation. This involves a role reversal: the theologian becoming first the one who learns.

Boff stresses the need for the irruption of the reality of poverty into the consciousness of the theologian. This is a prerequisite for a more social-analytical approach. Like Gutiérrez, he sees the theologian as an organic intellectual, but he seems to mean something different by this. Contact with the poor is an enrichment but not the seedbed of theology. Although he later explicitated three degrees of the option for the poor, he does not explicitly locate the theologian in this schema.

For Segundo, there is the clear assumption of involvement in the struggle, but, even more than for Boff, it is essentially at the level of a theoretic enrichment. Nonetheless, he suggests an inversion of the ordinary relation between social praxis and evangelical values as a precondition for the de-ideologization of the theological mind, stressing the hermeneutical importance of pretheological commitments. Nevertheless, while Segundo's theology enshrines the privilege of the poor, it is not rooted in them, nor does it seek to give them a foundational theological voice.

By implication, Sobrino seems to argue for a more rooted commitment. He frequently speaks of the exigency of "drawing near" to the poor. Discipleship is possible only if one's viewpoint is shaped by the poor. He resembles Gutiérrez and probably goes beyond him in stressing the poor as the *lugar teologico* of ecclesiology. They are less the recipients of theology than the condition of its possibility.

The Methodological Status of This Theological Project

Each of our authors accords the option for the poor a privileged status but there are differences of nuance in each case.

Metz's practical fundamental theology claims a hermeneutical privilege over "progressive theology" and privileges solidarity with the suffering over academic solidarity with the new "men of reason," by which he means the primacy of engaged reason over a putatively disinterested reason. His method involves demonstrating that the theological categories of memory, solidarity, and narrative are not merely precritical but strictly necessary to avoid reason degenerating into technique. This priority operates with a dialectical submission of theory to praxis and insists on reading history from the underside, thus privileging the experience of the suffering and abandoning argumentative competence as conclusive: Truth is more than competence.

If Metz is offering what is essentially a critical corrective to existing theology, Gutiérrez is proposing a totally different method. Henceforth, theology will be from the optic of the poor and will represent the right of the poor to think. Yet he does not make absolute and exclusivist claims for his hermeneutic. The theological model he proposes admits to needing traditional notions if only to refine them. He conceded in his earlier work that this method had not yet produced the necessary categories, was still in "first gear," and needed improvement. He defends his hermeneutical perspective by arguing that this is strictly necessary for scientific results and is not less serious for being closely bound up with commitment and struggle: The poor person as the revealer of the "utterly Other" is the departure point for theology.

Boff is equally adamant that the theological method under discussion is not just another genitive theology. The struggle for liberation from the perspective of the poor is the new horizon of theology. His fundamental theological argument is that the poor possess a sacramental function: Their rights are the rights of God, and thus the option for the poor is the starting point of theology. Boff stops short of any exclusivist claim. For him, every theology has limitations and none can claim a monopoly. His later work recognizes the distinction between the external practical and the internal theoretical fora of theology. Ultimately, it seems, he privileges his theological method on the basis of the exigencies of the present historical moment.

Segundo's principal contribution to this particular aspect of the question of the relative hermeneutical status of a theology elaborated out of an option for the poor has been his attempt to demonstrate that faith and ideology are inextricably interdependent. In this way, he has opened up theology to a systematic self-critical incorporation of ideology into its method. His theology makes an option for the poor in the sense of an engaged theoretic commitment. Any argument he would make for its methodological status seems to be implicit. His work assumes, takes for granted, indeed, that a theology of liberation is the most pertinent and realistic way to theologize. It seems to reject, however, its project of rooting theology in the poor themselves.

Sobrino develops the sacramental role of the poor to the extent of arguing that the mystery of God is accessible only to those who draw near to them. Echoing Gutiérrez's argument on the asymmetry of the word and deed and, even more so, Metz's, he seeks to justify theology not so much before the bar of reason as before the yearning for a transformative praxis. It is clear that for Sobrino the internal analytical elements of a theological method have less importance than the practical ethical options represented by the implicit model of understanding. Ultimately, Sobrino makes the greatest claim for a theology from the perspective of the poor. Linking his understanding of the revelation of the otherness of God in the otherness of the oppressed with his insistence that the epistemological break with natural reason demanded by the cross privileges a theological method that begins with the suffering, his argument not only elucidates the optic of the poor as an authentic theological source but claims for the option for the poor the source of any originality that theological science might claim.

Concluding Remarks

It is clear that a good deal of work remains to be done in establishing the relative status of the option for the poor as a hermeneutical perspective in theology. Indeed, not even the authors we have discussed are agreed as to what its status might be, much less as to how that might be established. It is the aim of the present work to make some contribution to such a project. This, in turn, demands that we examine the methodological assumptions that lie behind the adoption of the perspective of the option for the poor as well as spelling out the meaning and dimensions of this option for the theologian. But before that it will be necessary to explore the strengths and limitations of this theological perspective by considering several fundamental types of critique of this position, and that will be the material of our next chapter.

Notes

¹*The Community Called Church* (New York, 1975) 92.

²*Our Idea of God* (New York, 1977) 7–8.

³*The Liberation of Theology,* 86. Note Segundo's quite original development of the concept of ideology. It does not mean "false consciousness" but rationally chosen and empirically verifiable means to an end chosen on the basis of an antecedent values-option. Thus it is literally a "scientific" notion, i.e., verifiable: something not substantiated in relation to Marxism itself. On this usage he can employ aspects of e.g., Marxism as ideological, i.e., as analytical tools, while not accepting it as a worldview. Equally, ideology is chosen or adopted by faith in order to be historically effective. Operating at different levels, one in function of transcendent values, the other in function of historical efficacy, they are not only not incompatible but actually need each other.

⁴F. Engels to E. Bloch, September 21, 1890. Cf. *Marx and Engels: Selected Correspondence* (New York, 1942) 475. Cf. also V. I. Lenin, *What Is to Be Done* (New York, 1928) 41.

⁵*Faith and Ideologies* (New York, 1983) passim, esp. 26f., 31, 50, 95, 119f., 177f., 188, 247, 251f., 317f., cf. n. 3 above. In a similar vein, *see* J. Miranda, *Marx Against the Marxists* (New York, 1980).

⁶*The Historical Jesus of the Synoptics* (New York, 1986) 3, 12, 27, 77, 80, 118, 140.

[7]Ibid., 76.

[8]Ibid., 94.

[9]Ibid., 128.

[10]*The Humanist Christology of St. Paul* (New York, 1986) 10.

[11]Ibid., 173, 224, n. 254. Cf. *We Drink from Our Own Wells,* 126.

[12]Ibid., 174.

[13]*The Liberation of Theology,* 208–240; and *The Community Called Church,* 78–86.

[14]*The Humanist Christology of Paul,* 226, n. 262.

[15]J. Sobrino, *Cristología desde America Latina* (Mexico, 1976); English trans., *Christology at the Crossroads* (London, 1978). Cf. 124.

[16]This work is enormously influenced by Luther's theology of the cross as reinterpreted by Moltmann. This relativizes the somewhat extreme dichotomy Sobrino proposes between European and Latin American theology. It also relativizes one of Segundo's criticisms of Metz!

The original contribution is the development of the idea of seeing the otherness of God mediated through the otherness of the poor. But even this is seminally present in Bonhoeffer, as Gutiérrez has acknowledged. Nonetheless, one of the fundamental differences between European political theology and Latin American liberation theology remains, namely, the question of the theologian's own rootedness in the praxis of liberation within an option for the poor. For this is more than the "concept" of God suffering in the poor.

[17]Ibid., 348. Here Sobrino has touched upon an issue that is fundamental to what is being argued in the present work: the primacy of the perspective of the poor over that of disinterested cognition. We would qualify Sobrino's view. Cf. ch. 7.

[18]*The True Church of the Poor* (London, 1984) 9.

[19]Ibid., 52.

[20]Ibid., 93, 113. Thus, the elaboration of a theological method with the optic of the poor as its hermeneutical standpoint is not just one example of a local theology but a general methodological principle. We return to this in ch. 3. When Gutiérrez writes, "Gradually people are realizing that in the last resort it is not a question of the Church being poor, but of the poor of this world being the people of God" in "The Poor and the Church," Con 99 (1977) 11–16, he is expressing the same view. Both these writers are clearly different from Segundo. The Church does not just exist for the poor nor even especially for them but is rooted in them—as the kingdom is. *See also* Sobrino, "A Crucified People's Faith in the Son of God," Con 153 (1982) 23–28.

3

Facing the Basic Objections

Our next step toward more clearly defining the assumptions, limitations, strengths, and values of this theological perspective is not to consider every conceivable opinion on the topic but to attempt to subsume all the strands of critique under four headings: (A) the overtly hostile, (B) the constructively critical, (C) contextualization within a conversational model, and (D) qualification as local theology.

In this way, the present chapter will take the shape of resuming the principal arguments of four noteworthy works, each respectively offering a representative argument for the theological position under discussion. On the basis of a critique of these positions, we will have taken an important step forward in spelling out the strengths and limitations of a theological method elaborated from the perspective of an option for the poor.

The Overtly Hostile

According to the theological tendency under discussion here, a theology from the perspective of the poor, inasmuch as it were rooted in the historic praxis of liberation, would not be considered to be theology at all. We take as an example of this tendency a work of Juan Gutiérrez for the reason that from the very outset he "makes no bones about the critical intent of his study."[1] For him, the theology discussed in the previous chapters—as exemplified by G. Gutiérrez—would not be theology at all: "For him theology is not a theology of revelation but an understanding of 'praxis' which is never defined. It is praxis that carries the primacy and whatever he may say he can never escape from this contradiction. Finally, let me say that what he is setting out is not theology."[2]

This author begins by accusing Gutiérrez of an inaccurate use of sources, but we come closer to the kernel of his position when we note his opinion that Gutiérrez's account of what is permanent in the thought of Aquinas on theology as a rational science amounts to "an evaporation of the science of theology." There are two reasons for this opinion: the imputation to Gutiérrez of the views that the systematic explanation of truths has no permanent normative significance, and that theology is not an ancillary discipline to the ecclesiastical magisterium. Gutiérrez's project of organically linking sociology to theology is considered to mean the substitution of philosophy by sociology as the qualified representative of reason. With an implicit demand for conceptual exactitude within a given framework, our critic bemoans the absence of an acceptable definition of "historical praxis." The view that faith is an "overall attitude" is thus interpreted to mean the exclusion of the "cognitive element."

This allows the claim that the faith being proposed by Gutiérrez "is not the faith of the Bible which is why his theology lacks doctrinal content."[3] This theology, he suggests, is equally mistaken with regard to charity, for "it is not a matter of loving one's neighbor for whatever reason but because of the Lord." In the writer's view, Gutiérrez has not brought out the "primacy and the importance of the good of God." This is seen to derive from a misplacing of the principal *locus thelogicus*.

Further, in this writer's view, theology cannot be critical of itself and its basic principles, since these are the articles of faith. A theology of praxis contradicts theology's dependence on revelation.[4] Similarly, making faith depend both on praxis and the word is taken to imply yet another contradiction.

Beyond Theological Fundamentalism

The theological tendency exemplified in Juan Gutiérrez's work vehemently rejects a liberation theology from the perspective of the poor. Representing as it does one particularly attenuated understanding of the theological tradition, it is the one most threatened by the suggestion that an option for the poor rooted in the praxis of liberation affords a theological hermeneutical standpoint that is in some sense privileged. This sense of threat is evident from the manner in which he resorts to polemical language. G. Gutiérrez is accused of superficiality, contradictions, sophisms, distortions, and manipulations.[5] One might pass over this in silence were it not for the fact that what is at issue is the very notion of theological science. Throughout this work, the underlying assumption is that "theology" is substantially—if not completely —reducible to an already established body of premises and articles and that its method consists essentially in logical deductions from these. It would therefore be a methodologically unselfcritical science. Behind this rejection of Gutiérrez's demand that theology become self-critical stands the assumption that the nature and method of theology are definitively established, and thus any attempt to argue for a new hermeneutical standpoint in theology stands excluded *ab initio*. Needless to say, in the post-Modern era, which has abandoned the methodological naiveté of the first Enlightenment, this approach would leave theology open to the charge of being precritical and therefore unscientific.

Such a notion of theology is both fundamentalist and self-contradictory. It is fundamentalist in its design to identify tradition with a given stage in its development. It is self-contradictory because on these grounds the very classics of theology to which it seeks to give definitive status could themselves never have come into ecclesial acceptance—and nowhere is this more evident than in the case of Aquinas. To such an approach it matters little that the theological tradition is de facto an ongoing dialogue between successive breakthroughs. Not surprisingly, important contemporary developments such as revelation as history, theology as anthropology, the unity of the love of God and neighbor, and the methodological function of the hermeneutical circle—to say nothing of the question of a new interpretative horizon—find no acceptance here.

Yet the author has at least turned our attention to one fundamental question when he notes: "The real question is this: Does the theological concept of truth intrinsically include its particular historical efficacy?"[6]

For if theology seeks a purely cognitive truth within a logically coherent system divorced from the practical implications of either its presuppositions or its deductions, then the question of a hermeneutical perspective defined by an option for the poor—or indeed any practical commitment—becomes at best unimportant. Our own view is quite different. Theology clarifies the truth of faith, and this demands theoretical rigor and logical consistency *(fides quae creditur)*. But faith *(fides qua creditur)* is constitutively an existentially practical reality involving an option to live agapeistically and with historical responsibility. In this primordial sense, theology articulates a practical truth with a view to making it more evangelically practicable. The faith that seeks understanding through theology is not so much a set of concepts as a way of life. If theology is faith seeking understanding, then the ultimate aim of theological truth is a more informed and thereby more consistent faith praxis. The praxis of faith is the very space within which theological reflection operates, being both its source and its goal. But the praxis of faith is concerned with every dimension of God's salvific action, including the cultural, the social, and the process of history. Therefore, the concept of theological truth does include intrinsically its historical efficacy which is why the practical perspective of the theologian becomes a crucial question for theological method.

The Constructively Critical

As a paradigm of a second kind of critique of the project of constructing a theological hermeneutic based on the option for the poor as exemplified in chapters 1 and 2, we consider an important work of Clodovis Boff.[7] In terming this approach "constructively critical," we mean that his approach, within an essentially affirmative appraisal of liberation theology, attempts a critique of its methodological presuppositions and therefore of its epistemological status.

He is especially sensitive to the need to establish the strictly theological character *(teologicidade)* of any properly theological discourse, including a theology of the political. Despite the need to include the findings of the sociopolitical sciences in an organic way, this latter must remain theology.

It is not enough for liberation theologians merely to assert that they are doing theology in a new way. Their method, he holds, has remained at the level of repeating their assertions. It is now time to go beyond this first phase. His reference to the "intuitive and fragmentary character" of the methodological materials of the liberation theologians does, however, allow that there have been developments *"in acto exercito."*

He begins by placing liberation theology in the wider context of the theology of the political, and this in return is placed within the conjunction of what he terms *teologia um* (T1) and *teologia dois* (T2).[8] T1 is theology occupying itself directly with immediately religious topics—as in classical traditional theology. T2 is theology occupying itself directly with immediately secular realities. The essential difference is at the level of the thematic *(theologizandum)* and not the perspective *(theologizans)*. Unlike what sometimes appears to be the implicit position of the liberation theologians, T1 remains as an interpretative framework essential to the production of T2 and is thus constitutive of it. Hence the claim that "liberation" is the horizon from which to read the whole tradition of faith with the result that one is no longer involved in another "genitive theology" requires modification.

Sociopolitical reality is the material object of this theology, and specifically the theology of this social reality is its formal object. To each of these there corresponds a hermeneutical mediation: a social-analytical mediation (MSA) and a specifically theological hermeneutical mediation (MH). What is meant by "mediation" in this context is the conjunction of means that theology integrates in order to deal with its object. It is a *medium quo,* joined to theology not just technically but organically and thus internal to the theological enterprise.

Hermeneutical mediation, for example, through philosophical discourse, has always been emphatically asserted in Catholic theology in contradistinction to an extreme *sola fides* position. Our author may be regarded as simply extending this to argue that just as philosophical mediation is intrinsic to metaphysical theology, so are the fruits of the social sciences (CdS) constitutive of a theology that deals with a concrete sociopolitical reality. He is going beyond both the question of how theology can protect the social sciences from false hypotheses and the question of how these can enrich pastoral theology. Since the material theoretic object of the present theological exercise can be grasped only through the social sciences—unless one wishes to revert to a "common sense" position—then MSA is constitutive of theology, though not of faith per se.[9]

In evaluating the sometimes rather unnuanced way in which perspective is placed above thematic in some liberation theologies, this writer introduces the distinction that in relation to praxis, theology is both "autonomous" and "dependent." "Autonomy" refers to theology's internal structuring, its immanent logic. "Dependency" refers to theology's organic insertion in a practical multiform relation of function. While this is organically related to theology and thus part of it, it cannot per se—no more than any sociopolitical destination—establish the quality of its theoretic status. We too would wish to avoid such a theoretic pragmatism. While we seek to argue that the option for the poor is, in principle, a relatively privileged hermeneutical perspective, we do not suggest that all theologians attempting to theologize from this perspective necessarily produce good theology. This qualification, however, does not allow theology to pursue its project in solely intellectualist terms, implying as it would, a naive voluntarism that would ascribe to theology a power of personal and social transformation it might not possess.

Having established the constitutive importance of social-analytical hermeneutical mediation, Clodovis Boff then turns to the more immanently theological task. He first sets out to include theological thinking into a generalized picture of the process of theoretic practice on the grounds that theological thinking is homologous with all systematic thinking. Here he follows Althusser's[10] tripartite distinction between what is known and in some sense grasped, though in need of cognitive transformation (G1); the means of producing this transformed known, that by which G1 is elaborated, that is, a theory or body of concepts (G2); and that which is thereby produced—a body of knowledge more concrete, specific, and scientific (G3), the production of which involves a genuine *rupture epistemologique*. Everything is theological and thus a *theologizandum* (G1). What makes theology to be theology is the *rationem secundum quam considerantur* (G2). Thus, in Aquinas' terms, these (G2) are the *articuli fidei*[11] by means of which one theologizes. But since this positivity of faith is both a process of cognitive transformation and the product of one, it in turn demands that the hermeneutical process of producing it be examined.

This mediation refers first to the necessary relation of a theology of sociopolitical reality to the Christian sources, which of course give it its identity. MSA and MH are both constitutive of theology but not in the same way. MSA is the G1, which operated on by MH, acting as G2, produces TdP, which is the G3. In observing how this hermeneutical operation is elaborated, care must be taken to find the right point of insertion in the various hermeneutical circles that define the relationship between reading the sources and reading in the light of the sources.

Hermeneutically speaking, the construction of a theology from the perspective of the oppressed mirrors the process of the New Testament in a creative fidelity both to Jesus—as in the tradition—and to later developments. The fundamental identity of meaning is neither at the level of context—for the context both of Jesus and of the New Testament is different from the contemporary problematic of poverty and oppression—nor at the level of content—for simply to repeat the words of Jesus, something the New Testament itself does not do, would be fundamentalism—but at the level of the relation between these two. In this way a genuine equivalence of significance *(homosemeia)* can be achieved between the past meaning of Scripture and the present meaning of the historical situation.

A Methodological Advance

This approach has succeeded in exploring some of the strengths and weaknesses of a theology operating from the perspective of the poor as exemplified in chapters 1 and 2. In particular, it has shown that the mere claim to operate with "liberation," or indeed any other praxis-based perspective as the horizon of understanding, is insufficient per se to establish the strictly theological character of the enterprise. Even though all reality is theological in the sense of potentially revealing God—whose self-revelation is coextensive with history—nonetheless, what establishes an enterprise as theological is the interpretative framework, the *rationem secundum quam considerantur*. In the present instance, this calls for a strictly theological meaning of the option for the poor and of liberation.

This means that the claim of liberation theology to be not just another genitive theology must be qualified. Since the hermeneutical standpoint for the understanding of the fruits of MSA can only be supplied by theology as it exists, on this half of the hermeneutical circle the new theology remains a genitive theology. Theology—T1—will, of course, be internally reconstructed as a consequence of this operation.

Equally valuable is the distinction between the internal-autonomous and the external-dependent fora of theology. Not least, it helps one understand how a theologian who makes the option for the poor can conceivably produce "bad" theology, while some theologians on the "margins of the struggle" can produce "good" theology. Seen in this light, Sobrino's prioritizing of motivational interest over internal method could run the risk of theoretical pragmatism, even though this is quite absent from his own work.

Establishing the organically constitutive function of social-analytical mediation is a major contribution to a question that has been debated for some time concerning Christian sociopolitical thinking as a third way between individualism and collectivism. It leaves behind the naive and ultimately unhelpful approach of a social ethic derived directly from the traditional texts—a process that is ideologically unself-critical. By demonstrating the necessity of incorporating the fruits of social analysis, it accepts being consciously though self-critically ideological, while looking to the tradition for the basis of the antecedent ethical option governing the choice of analytical model.

As a result, the theological method operative in the examples discussed in the previous chapters is vindicated precisely as theology, while the methodological claims of theologians operating from the perspective of an option for the poor will, in the light of this work, be more modest, but they will also be more firmly based.

Contextualization Within a Conversational Model

A third kind of critique of the view that the option for the poor, or indeed any particular perspective, enjoys a hermeneutical privilege in theology is argued in the conversational model of D. Tracy.[12] Theology's criteria of adequacy must, for Tracy, correspond to the highest standards of the modern academy. But the theologian is also a member of a Church and of a society, and so his work is related to the plausibility structures of all three. Thus, he is led to speak of a tripartite distinction within theology, making it not a single discipline but three: fundamental, systematic, and practical theology, or, to use his own term, the "three publics of the theologian."

Tracy argues that these three theologies each have (A) distinct primary reference groups, (B) distinct modes of argument, (C) distinct understandings of the theologian's ethical stance, (D) distinct understandings of the theologian's personal faith, and (E) distinct formulations of what counts as meaning and truth.

He sees practical theology as a mediated theology grounded in the transformative praxis of the authentic intellectual and the community. It has a wide range due to different interpretations of the notion of praxis, different historical circumstances, and different prophetic stances. Anticipating a later discussion in the present work, Tracy points to the Gadamer-Habermas debate as illustrating the theory-praxis problematic in contemporary theology: the former arguing for the disclosive power of the Greek tradition, the latter that in a society of systematically distorted communication, rhetoric is powerless.[13]

Tracy warns against a dichotomization of "disclosure" and "transformation" criteria of truth to the detriment of the comprehensive notion of rationality operative in both. Equally, the shift to socioethical concern in theology does not dissipate the crisis of cognitive claims. The need for argumentation, abstraction, and the ideal of conversation remain.

Conversation is the key concept: The common journey to the truth of the three theologies is not by way of confrontation, much less by reinventing the "canon within the canon," but by way of the Gadamerian notion of conversation, of which the Platonic dialogue is the exemplar. Here the dialogue goes beyond the need for self-justification into a truly joint reflection given over to the priority of the question.[14]

The context of the ensuing discussion in Tracy's work is the notion of the theologian as the interpreter of the religious classic. This classic is viewed as that which paradigmatically mediates the disclosure-concealment of the whole by the power of the whole; the interpretative theory is essentially Gadamerian. Locating practical and liberation theologies in this schema, Tracy takes the liberation theologians much more seriously than in his previous work. Nonetheless, he seems to relativize their importance, stressing what he considers to be M. Eliade's prophetic role in challenging the dominant prophetic-ethical-historical trajectory of Western religion in favor of its grounds in the power of manifestation.

The interpreter must pay attention to the conversational interdependence of the literary-critical, the historical-critical, and the social-scientific, offering and receiving correctives at each level. As an application of this conversational balance, he proposes that for a classic expression of the New Testament, we see both apocalyptic and early Catholicism as corrective. Similarly, it is not necessary to decide between proclamation and narrative as the primary New Testament genre. Interpretation must remain open to all genuine developments as well as do justice to the complex reality of the interpreter's keeping the individual, interpersonal, and structural dimensions in view. Interpretation, to be adequate to the actual situation, must take seriously the responsibility of the self to all reality, especially the poor. But for Tracy, this admittedly real privileged status of the oppressed is not equivalent to a hermeneutical principle of interpretation: he demands that liberation hermeneutics remain within a wider conversation of all interpreters.

A "criterion of relative adequacy" is an attempt to be faithful to the range of disclosures in the New Testament with a concomitant fidelity to one's situation. In this manner "analogical imagination" can be operative. By this, Tracy means "an intensified journey into a particularity that is accompanied by a willing self-exposure to the concreteness of the whole."[15]

The theologian is faced, according to Tracy, with an absence of consensus as to what is the central interpretation or the central question. In this regard, where he differs fundamentally from those who spontaneously take up the issue of poverty and oppression, Tracy sees the effect of the "masters of suspicion"[16] on the pretensions of conscious rationality. He asks us to look at three distinct foci of meaning of the event of Jesus: manifestation, proclamation, and historical action, arguing that any consequent pluralism is not an invention of the age but a reality in all the traditions. He allows that the loyalty of liberation theologians is to God's own privileged ones, that they can identify "the question" of our times—the "massive catastrophic suffering of whole peoples." Further, he concedes that their theological method, because it is more established, has become self-critical, becoming less confrontational and thereby allowing "the real theological conflict of mutually respecting argument to occur."[17]

So Tracy remains qualified in his appraisal; for him it remains a theology in search of a classic text. He is nonetheless prepared to admit that these theologies do allow theologians to hear the tradition from a perspective faithful to its innermost self-understanding: that perspective privileged both by the prophets and by Jesus himself.

Against this backdrop he returns to his chosen model of conversation following analogical imagination. Dialectic and analogy need each other to prevent the one from becoming univocity and compromise and the other from exploding into rage and despair: any claim to final adequacy masks a manipulative spirit. Once focal meaning is chosen, the interpretative journey can begin, but the understanding will be transformed through exposure to a fuller range of meanings. The three foci of manifestation, proclamation, and historical action both clarify and intensify—and occasionally distort—some major aspect or emphasis in the originating event. The need for all three remains: each theology remains faithful to its chosen paradigm but open to the fullness of the whole, and the collaborative character of theology will ensure that the ensuing conversation will not be allowed to stop too soon.

Balance or Transformation

The systematic analogical imagination of Tracy is essentially a process of dynamic conversational balance. But if we are to have balance, then where shall we place the fulcrum? Even if truth is also (as distinct from "only" or even "primarily") practical and transformational as well as theoretical and disclosive, then balance and conversation are equally practical achievements. The accepted plausibility structures of academy, Church, and society always imply a preference and prioritizing in the concrete: theoretical resolution is often only at the conceptual level.

Frequently, the privilege of the oppressed is emphasized, but this, it is alleged, does not imply a hermeneutical privilege. This is partly explained by the implicit hermeneutical tendencies of the work, which tacitly favor a conceptual understanding of theology over a practical one, despite the fact that Tracy has left behind many of the reservations expressed in *Blessed Rage for Order*.[18] Although the theologian is repeatedly reminded that he is one who also interprets the contemporary reality, there is no attempt to demarcate the great practical issues of this historical moment, nor even to outline the criteria upon which this might be done. This evaluation seems supported by Tracy's apparent preference for the mystical-metaphysical-aesthetic over the ethical-prophetic-historical in religious disclosure as well as his virtually neo-Bultmannian position on the historical Jesus.

The systematic-fundamental-practical distinction is also valuable, but it needs to face the question of the relationship, in principle and in practice, between the three. All theologies have practical consequences as well as a practical inner moment. Practical theology—certainly in the present case of a theology elaborated from the perspective of an option for the poor—equally intends to be both systematic and fundamental.

In presenting the conversation between New Testament genres as isomorphic with the conversation between theologies, the same question arises: Does each operate as a corrective on the other in precisely the same way? Does *Fruehkatholicismus* correct apocalyptic in a manner that is symmetric with apocalyptic's corrective function in relation to the whole tradition? Indeed, even Tracy's own use of apocalyptic,[19] would seem to concur with the present writer's view of allowing it the role of "major internal corrective." Is there not a similar asymmetry in the interrelationships between Tracy's three theologies?

Nonetheless, the dialogical ideal is irreplaceable: the truth is attained in the to-and-fro of the self-correcting, mutually enriching process of theological conversation. Nonpractical theologies have produced classics without which there could be no theological dialogue worthy of the name. But every theologian is standing somewhere: Like it or not, he or she favors some conversation partners above others, and Tracy's work implicitly favors the academy. The perspective of the academy is a necessary corrective to the perspective of the oppressed, just as it needs this corrective in return. But just as in the case of apocalyptic, the process is not symmetrical—though we have still to establish this.

Local Theology or Quasi-Invariant Methodological Principle

A fourth kind of critique of the thesis of the hermeneutical privilege of the option for the poor is implicit in the work of R. Schreiter.[20] This writer has sought to systematize recent missiological developments by elaborating the structures of what he terms "local theologies." In this scheme a theology from the perspective of the poor may be said to be one possible expression of a local theology. Such local theologies involve a dialogue between local context, experience, and history on the one hand and the lived tradition of the Church on the other. He argues for a theological model that begins with an examination of context rather than the application of the existing model to the context. Thus, in a context where issues of oppression are paramount, theology might begin with an analysis of power relationships. Schreiter is arguing for an approach that surpasses translation and adaptation models with contextual models, distinguishing among the latter those emphasizing identity from those emphasizing transformation in what he terms "ethnocentric approaches" and "liberation approaches."[21] The former takes identity seriously but risks overlooking conflictual factors for the sake of identity in harmony. The latter are, for Schreiter, the major force in contextual models of theology today.

Equally basic to this view is the shift to the community as the subject of theology, Solentiname being an outstanding example. Since faith is communitarian, so is theology; it is not the property of the theologian class. The community's "reception" of the faith includes an active and creative role in shaping and articulating it. The professional theologian has an indispensable role, but it is one of organic linkage to and service of the faith experience of the community, which is the *locus theologicus*.

If a community is the subject of a local theology, it is equally its audience. Schreiter adopts Tracy's tripartite distinction with regard to the "public" of theology, stressing the importance of one's awareness of who the intended audience is. An academic theology, he insists, does not have an implicit superiority.

He recognizes that attention solely to the dimensions of identity formation, group bonding, and worldview can leave cultural analysis unable to deal with the dynamics of change because of an unwitting commitment to current power relations. This problem is particularly evident where a functionalist approach is employed.[22] Structuralist approaches can also indicate certain possible trajectories of change, but their reliance on structures of mind make them, in their own way, just as reductionist as a materialist reading.

One of the strengths of a local theology is its grasp of the fact that understanding is deeply influenced by cultural context. Theology is embedded in culture and takes on cultural forms. Its self-understanding can benefit from a modest use of the sociology of knowledge, for the latter can at least partially indicate the connectedness of the growth and decline of certain theological ideas with their social contexts, despite the fact that a totally exhaustive description is rarely possible. Thus a sociology of theology, in indicating how forms of theological thought are related to certain cultural conditions, can also help us to evaluate assertions by one or the other group who protests that a given work is not theology at all.

Schreiter attempts to show how theology, constituted respectively as variations on a text, wisdom, *scientia,* and as praxis, is elaborated in function of different sociocultural conditions. Displaying a keen understanding of political theology and the scope of liberation, he states: "The Latin American liberation theologians have become the best known although liberation theology is not all of the same type. The nature of social oppression will reshape the focus from place to place. In some instances an analysis along the lines of class is most enlightening. This has been the case in much of Latin America. In other cases the issue is race. . . . Praxis arising from reflection along lines of sex is found among women on several continents. Or again the factor can be religious language or caste."[23]

But our author still seems to localize liberation theology as arising "in those areas among the people who are oppressed." "The oppressor" he notes, "will use a different method." He even wonders if this method of theologizing could be sustained "once liberation is achieved." It is, he adds, less successful for sustaining identity.

Schreiter seeks to make an analogy with Chomsky's model of language acquisition.[24] Tradition would be the analogue of the entire language system, with faith analogous to linguistic competence and theology to performance. The loci of grammar in Christian tradition would be the loci of orthodoxy. By continuing the analogy, he can argue that theology can no more flow from the loci of orthodoxy than language performance can from grammar. Magisterial theology, despite its validity, can never be the theology of a community: To make it such would be like attempting to derive idiom from grammar.

Option for the Poor: A Universal Issue

In this schema, a theological method privileging the optic of the poor would appear as one example—among many—of a local theology. Schreiter's work goes a long way toward validating much of what we would wish to say about a theology from the side of the oppressed, and this theology receives considerable underpinning from his contention—adequately argued—that the tradition is a series of local theologies and that orthodoxy is the grammar rather than the idiom of theology. He has also demonstrated that there have always been local theologies because of the cultural embeddedness of theology and that the tradition—implicitly or explicitly—has always granted greater normativity to some theologies than to others. He has also explained how a theological method must be judged according to its proper criteria.

In demonstrating that the community is itself the subject of a local theology, he reminds us that the theologian who makes the option for the poor does not impose his own theological agenda.

Where Schreiter differs from the present work is that we are attempting to examine the option for the poor as a methodological perspective for any theological enterprise. We are thus going beyond the position where it arises quasi-spontaneously in function of a particular set of sociocultural conditions. Our contention is that the distinction he draws between identity and change —while soundly based in cultural anthropology—and the relative weight he gives to each, does not do justice to a specifically Christian community whose identity is found precisely in the ongoing change that is conversion to the incarnate Lord in the least of his brethren. Since all human structures are characterized by power relations giving rise to marginalization and oppression, it is important to ask, as Sobrino does, about the cultural conditions correlative to theology as liberative praxis. It may be that the optic of the poor will not be sustained in some particular situations after a given degree of liberation. Equally, it is beyond question that many theological reflections are elaborated from other perspectives. Under these conditions, however, an effort must be made to see if and to what extent religion is being made to operate as a legitimation mechanism for the social order in which it finds itself. Inculturation, crucial though it be, does not exhaust the exigencies of evangelization, and one need only look to those parts of the world where Christianity seems most inculturated to see the point. The hermeneutical perspective afforded to theology through the option for the poor seeks precisely to protect theology from becoming a fellow traveler in oppression, as well as to direct its gaze toward those groups who live at the underside of history. In the latter sense, "the poor are always with us"—even in our affluence.

In practice, not all local theologies privilege the perspective of the poor. But in principle, all are open to being enriched by being reminded that the tradition of which they are a part privileges the little ones. The professional theologian, organically linked to the local community, is in a particularly strong position to mediate this. Where oppression, injustice, or marginalization are perceived issues, there may be different localized theologies, each privileging the perspective of an addressed group, operating on the basis of the perspective of the poor, and affording a relatively privileged hermeneutical standpoint. But the issue of the poor is a universal issue even when it is not perceived to be such. Theology elaborated from the perspective of the poor can no more be characterized simply as a local theology than can the question of the poor be characterized as a local issue.

Concluding Remarks

Only a theological fundamentalism would deny that the theological project under discussion is truly theology. An occasional unnuanced claim to be a totally new theological method without reference to the previous tradition is something of a shortcoming, but it would be quite unfair to generalize at this point or not to point out that there is an ongoing process of refinement for a theology that is still in "first gear." The scope of the methodological principle under investigation is universal; the different modalities that express it in a given contextualization are local. The question of its relative normative status remains thus far unresolved. Given the dialogical nature of theology, it cannot make an absolute or exclusivist claim. The issue hinges on the possibility of a privileged hermeneutic, and it is to this question that we must address ourselves, having first explored more adequately the main methodological assumptions of the position being adopted. Previous to that, we need to make a more comprehensive statement as to what we interpret the option for the poor to mean for the theologian. But first we must pause to consider two important Vatican documents.

Notes

[1] *Teología de la Liberación: Evaporación de la Teología.* English trans., *The New Libertarian Gospel: The Pitfalls of Liberation Theology* (Chicago, Franciscan Herald Press, 1977) xi. In the same vein cf. G. Cottier, *Difficultés d'une Théologie de la Liberation* (Paris, 1974); A. Lopez Trujillo, *Teología Libertadora en América Latina* (Bogota, 1974); R. Vekemans, *Caesar and God* (Orbis, 1972).

[2] *The New Libertarian Gospel,* 37.

[3] Ibid., 47. Cf. 30-31, 78.

[4] Ibid., 82, 87. This author needs to "recall also that while the articles of faith serve as the first principles of theological science, they are in themselves as propositions no more ultimate than are the first principles of reason; . . . what is revealed is God, not a set of propositions. Systematic theology makes even less claims to cage divine truth than systematic philosophy to capture the essence of material things." T. Gilbey, *Summa Theologiae; Vol. 1 (1a1); Christian Theology* (London and New York, 1963) 115-116.

[5] *The New Libertarian Gospel,* 47, 75, 85.

[6] Ibid., 14.

[7] C. Boff, *Teologia e Prática: Teologia do Político e suas Mediações* (Petropolis, 1978); English trans., *Theology and Praxis* (New York, 1987).

[8] *Teologia e Prática,* 32. For consistency, we follow C. Boff's system of abbreviations: MSA = social-analytical mediation; MH = hermeneutical mediation, which—somewhat imprecisely—refers here to that horizon of understanding that is specifically theological; CdS = social sciences; TdP = theology of the political (distinguished from "political theology" to highlight the formal object, cf. p. 27), as well as T1 and T2 already explained in the text. G1, G2, and G3; G = Generalité (Althussar), "generality" because knowledge refers to universals and not just to the singular and concrete. Cf. ST q. 86 a1 c. It is not clear to us why Clodovis Boff chooses to depend on Althussar, given the latter's questionable philosophy of science (cf. Merquior, *Western Marxism,* 148). Boff could have made the same point by reference to Aquinas: cf. ST 1 q 1, a 7, R. "Quidam vero, attendentes ea quae tractatur in ista scientia (G1) et non ad rationem secundum quam (G2) considerantur, assignaverunt aliter materiam huius scientiae. . . . "

⁹*Teologia e Prática,* 43, 46.

¹⁰L. Althussar, *Pour Marx* (Paris, 1965) 186–197; also *Lire le Capital* (Paris, 1973) 1:46–50; cf. n. 8 above.

¹¹ST 1, q 1, 8, R, "ita haec doctrina non argumentatur ad sua principia probanda, quae sunt articuli fidei, sed ex eis procedit ad aliquid ostendendum. . . . "

¹²D. Tracy, *The Analogical Imagination: Christian Theology and the Culture of Pluralism* (London, 1981).

¹³We will deal with the Gadamer-Habermas debate in detail in ch. 9. We take the opposing view to Tracy. To be more precise, we feel that Tracy has not followed the implications of his opinion that "Gadamer is insufficiently sensitive to the occasional need (personally and societally) for the kinds of ideology critique provided by the great hermeneutes of suspicion, Freud, Marx and Nietzsche." He adds that Gadamer's achievement is "in danger of becoming an unconsciously retrospective Utopia." *Analogical Imagination,* 137, n. 16. It is difficult to see how one can hold this view without adopting Habermas' perspective. *See also* ch. 10.

¹⁴Tracy frequently cites Gadamer; it would scarcely be an oversimplification to describe his work as an attempted theological transposition of Gadamer's hermeneutics. While accepting the point that both Gadamer and Tracy make, we must qualify it with reference to the sociopolitical conditions under which the Platonic dialogues emerged. K. R. Popper in *The Open Society and its Enemies,* vol. 1, *The Spell of Plato* (London, 1974), has shown that Plato's state was a caste state (p. 46) and that Plato was opposed to the abolitionist movement (pp. 45, 224), placing the rights of property above slaves (p. 221). Popper notes how Plato adopts a propagandist attitude by not using the term "slaves" (p. 47). Against egalitarian currents, he advanced—as did Aristotle— the theory of biological inequality, making the slave-master distinction "natural" (p. 70). In making these observations, we are anticipating our remarks on the sociopolitical rootedness of thought—and theology (ch. 7)—as well as on our discussion on "systematically distorted communication" (ch. 10). We are not taking from Plato's achievement—nor, by extrapolation, from that of "traditional theology." We are, rather, simply noting that they are neither neutral nor innocent.

¹⁵*The Analogical Imagination,* 312.

¹⁶This is P. Ricoeur's phrase for the impact of Marx, Freud, and Nietzsche on post-Modern consciousness. Cf. P. Ricoeur, *The Conflict of Interpretations* (Evanston, 1974) 148–150.

¹⁷*The Analogical Imagination,* 397. However, E. Dussel, in "Theologies of the Periphery and the Centre: Encounter or Confrontation?" Con 171:1 (1984) 87–94, takes a less "conciliatory" view, speaking of "distance" and "negation" and arguing that theology from the periphery "will require a complete and total rereading of the whole of theology." Dussel makes the point but hardly establishes it. We may add that Tracy's theological conversation is itself conducted at the "center."

¹⁸*Blessed Rage for Order* (New York, 1975).

¹⁹*The Analogical Imagination,* 293, n. 54. "Readers will note that my own theological use of the genre of apocalyptic agrees far more with those of Metz and Moltmann in its emphasis on the negations of present reality."

²⁰R. Schreiter, *Constructing Local Theologies* (New York, 1985).

²¹Ibid., 13.

²²Ibid., 44; cf. p. 44, nn. 6 and 7. This discussion may be considered a parallel in anthropology to the discussion on hermeneutics that we take up in ch. 9.

[23]Ibid., 95f., 33.

[24]Ibid., 114. Schreiter is drawing on N. Chomsky, *Aspects of a Theory of Syntax* (Cambridge, Mass., 1965). Chomsky reversed the priority of grammar over idiom. Grammar becomes descriptive rather than determinative of the rules of the language; it mediates between competence and performance. "Competence" is a hypothesis governed by grammar; idiomatic "performances" can change "grammar."

4

The Praxis of Liberation and the Congregation for the Doctrine of the Faith

Because many of the works and opinions under discussion in this chapter refer to liberation theology rather than specifically to a theology elaborated from the perspective of the poor, a certain clarification of terms is called for.

By "liberation theology" we understand the theological tendency that lies behind our discussions in the first two chapters of the present work. We understand it as a theological method in function of the liberation of the poor and oppressed—and in interpreting the latter we avoid any spiritualizing tendency. There are other localized variants on liberation theology, for example, feminist, black, ethnic, linguistic. We regard these as valid but subordinate uses of the term liberation, applicable inasmuch as such groups may in a given historical circumstance be oppressed. Equally, there could be forms of feminist, black, ethnic, or linguistic "liberation" that do not seek a transformation of society from the perspective of the poor but rather equality within the status quo. Such "liberation theologies" would not be operating, in the full sense, from the hermeneutical perspective of the oppressed.

Nontheless, the perspective of the poor always includes the dimension of liberation, because in analyzing the phenomena of poverty and oppression it seeks to uncover the underlying structural causes. Moreover, acquiring the perspective of the poor includes the task of empowering the poor to be themselves the agents of liberation and the main protagonists in the struggle for a new communitarian way of life that more adequately reflects the Trinitarian community of God. Participation in the praxis of liberation is an integral part of the option for the poor. Thus, while liberation theology may not be simply identified with a theology from the perspective of the poor, since this latter includes dimensions other than the liberation struggle, a critique of the fundamentals of liberation theology would be an implicit critique of a theology from the perspective of an option for the poor.

Libertius Nuntius

This long-awaited *Instruction on Certain Aspects of the "Theology of Liberation"*[1] agrees that the Christian meaning of liberation is receiving "a new kind of attention which is itself full of promise." It notes, however, that "some are tempted to emphasize unilaterally the liberation . . . of an earthly . . . kind." Remarking that theologians "make use of different concepts without sufficient critical caution," it specifies its "limited and precise purpose": "To draw attention to the deviations and risk of deviations damaging to the faith and to Christian living that are brought about by certain forms of liberation theology which use in an insufficiently critical manner concepts borrowed from various currents of Marxist thought." The text, however, continues: "This warning should in no way be interpreted as a disavowal of all those who want to respond generously and with an authentic evangelical spirit to the preferential option for the poor. It should not at all serve as an excuse for those who maintain an attitude of neutrality in the face of . . . injustice."[2]

Allowing that liberation is a Christian theme, it states, though without any examples or clarification, that "as with all movements of ideas, the theologies of liberation present diverse theological positions." Nonetheless, the document allows that "in itself . . . theology of liberation is a thoroughly valid term," adding that "it designates a theological reflection centered on the biblical theme of liberation" (3.3), though without mention of any hermeneutical perspective from which this reflection might be conducted.

In considering the biblical foundation for liberation, the text emphasizes liberation from sin but in a manner that seems to divorce both sin and liberation from sin from the concrete reality of human experience. In considering liberation theology's emphasis on the Exodus, it argues, in parallel vein, that "the specific significance of the event comes from its purpose, for this liberation is ordered to the foundation of the people of God and the Covenant cult celebrated on Mount Sinai." Quoting Jeremiah only in terms of a "conversion of hearts," the text alludes to the prophetic vigor of Amos only to argue that as realized in the New Testament, "conversion and renewal have to occur in the depths of the heart." That the poor of the Beatitudes are in fact the actually materially poor, who are also spiritually poor in their longing and dependence on God to inaugurate God's reign of graciousness in contradiction to the present order, finds insufficient echo here. In any comparison of the structural and personal components of the human condition, the former are presented as largely consequential. "Structures whether they are good or bad are the result of man's actions and so are consequences more than causes" (4.15).

The instruction resumes the magisterial teaching since *Mater et magistra,* making "special mention" (5.7)—by implication, agreement and approval—of Medellín and Puebla. Reacting against any equation of salvation with solely politico-economic freedom, it sees "the different theologies of liberation situated between the 'preferential option for the poor' forcefully reaffirmed without ambiguity after Medellín at the conference of Puebla, on the one hand and the temptation to reduce the Gospel to an earthly gospel on the other" (6.5). The argument then moves on to a statement, the understanding of which is crucial for the overall significance of the instruction: "In this present document we will be discussing developments of that current of thought which under the name of the theology of liberation proposes a novel interpretation of God, the content of faith and of Christian existence which seriously departs from the faith of the Church and in fact, actually constitutes a practical negation" (6.9).

"Concepts uncritically borrowed from Marxist ideology" and "a biblical hermeneutic marked by rationalism" are seen to be the basis of this new interpretation. According to the document, Christians have turned to Marxist analysis because of "impatience and a desire for results" (7.1). They have done so uncritically, since "the borrowing of a method of approach to reality should be preceded by a careful epistemological critique. This preliminary critical study is missing from more than one theology of liberation." The view of Marxism communicated by the instruction is rather monolithic: It is "a global vision of reality" whose "ideological structure predetermines the significance and importance" of all data. According to the instruction, "no separation of the parts of this epistemologically unique complex is possible. If one tries to take only one part, say the analysis, one ends up having to accept the entire ideology" (7.6).

Marxism, in ignoring the limitations deriving from science, results in the "subversion of the meaning of the truth," the inseparability of "analysis" and praxis, the only true consciousness being a "partisan consciousness," with no access to truth "except in and through the partisan praxis." Since praxis is characterized by "class struggle," "truth is a truth of class: there is no truth but the truth in the struggle of the revolutionary class." This is seen as leading to a doctrine of necessary violence and political amorality, denying the transcendent character of ethics.[3]

This interpretation is then applied in some detail: "Class struggle" divides the Church; affirming one history is "historicist immanentism"; the theological virtues are "emptied of their theological meaning" (9.2). Liberation theology is seen as making "a disastrous confusion between the poor of sacred Scripture and the proletariat of Marx," making the Church of the people a "Church of class" which becomes a "challenge to the sacramental and hierarchical structure of the Church" (9.9).

There is a call to justice, but addressed, apparently, only at the individual level. The document asks us "not to lose sight of the fact that the source of injustice is in the hearts of men. Therefore it is only by making an appeal to the moral potential of the person and the constant need for interior conversion that social change will be brought about which will truly be in the service of man" (10.2).

The rejection of a structural-analytical approach which, we argue, is a constitutive dimension of the option for the poor, is characterized by what is termed the "inversion of morality and structures," holding it to be a "fatal illusion to believe that these new structures will of themselves give birth to a new man" (11.9).

Reading the Instruction

There are four major difficulties involved in evaluating this instruction. These are as follows:

1. The general terms in which it is couched; no theologians are named. Reference is not made to specific works.

2. The ordinary difficulties in theologically evaluating a statement from a Roman Congregation.

3. The special difficulties that arise from its similarities—of tenor and text—with previously published nonmagisterial books and interviews.[4]

4. The procedural difficulty in deciding on the structure of the text. Should it be seen as a composite whole essentially hostile to liberation theology and, therefore, by implication, to the project of a theological hermeneutic rooted in the option for the poor—in the sense being argued in this work? Should it be read as containing two quite distinct parts, the first, up to section 6.9, accepting of liberation theology in principle; the second (6.10f.), dismissive of "certain aspects," that is, essentially those aspects thought to borrow Marxist concepts uncritically?

Segundo feels profoundly affected by the document and sees in it a rejection of his theological method. He notes what he terms a seesaw effect between the odd- and even-numbered chapters but argues strongly that the document be seen as a composite whole, finding it "hermeneutically unsound and unfaithful to take its positive elements (in the odd-numbered chapters) out of their obvious and explicitly 'negative' context and thus 'save' the theology of liberation."[5]

He finds even in the first section a particular theology built on a kind of "textbook Platonism," a supposition that "sin as a religious reality is a totally adequate explanation" of all concrete social evil. By making a radical separation between liberation from sin and liberation of a "temporal kind," it seems to bring theology back to a "distinction of planes" model with its implied assumption that unlike liberation theology, it is not subject to ideological infiltration. An example of this would be the anachronistic use of "redemption" in its current religious sense as a synonym for "freedom"[6] in its contemporary secular sense.

As compelling as these arguments are, we do not follow them to the extent of seeing in the document an utter and total rejection of liberation theology and, by implication, of the hermeneutical perspective being proposed here—and this for four reasons:

1. Prima facie there are two parts to the instruction, one accepting in principle of liberation theology, the other dismissive of the employment of Marxist analysis and its consequences. Studies of the structure and genesis of the text support this view.

2. The theology implicit in the first section cannot possibly be construed to be the only legitimate Catholic theology. There is a legitimate plurality of theologies within the Church—as there is in the New Testament.

3. We should recognize that the instruction does explicitly recognize the legitimacy of liberation theology and specifically states that it wishes to deal with "deviations." Even its title refers not to liberation theology per se but to "certain aspects." This interpretation finds support in the declaration of the Peruvian episcopacy, which not only refused to condemn Gutiérrez but responded to the instruction in the way being proposed here.[7]

4. The text pointedly rules out a "disavowal" of all "those who want to respond generously and with an authentic evangelical spirit to the 'preferential option for the poor.' " Seeking to make this option the sentient base of a theological reflection and further seeking to establish the resulting hermeneutic's relative status is the methodological correlative of this response.

The crucial point therefore is the question of the use of certain aspects of Marxist thought and analysis as pre-theological tools, and it is to this question that we now turn.

Marxist Analysis in Christian Theology

Critical use of Marxist categories is possible not only on the basis of a theological *Aufhebung* but also because twentieth-century Marxism is itself self-critical. Certainly there is an "official Marxism," namely, that enunciated at and in continuity with the Third International. Ironically, when this functioned as the official ideology of the USSR, it did so precisely in the sense critiqued by Marx himself.[8] The sheer economism in the developing official line had already been criticized by Engels in his lifetime, and with the rediscovery of the *Fruehschriften* and the humanism of the "early Marx," two currents are clearly discernible. Indeed, what has become known as "Western Marxism" is essentially a humanistic critique of official Marxism. It is precisely this critique with its roots in the works of Bloch and Gramsci that has influenced political and liberation theologies. Bloch's "warm stream" is a very different interpretation of reality from Lenin's economism. The incorporation of the humanism of B. Croce into Gramsci's "Italian Marxism" laid the groundwork for a Eurocommunism that would eventually abandon the "dictatorship of the proletariat." The debate continued in recent French Communism between R. Garaudy and L. Althusser.[9] Certainly, the instruction has recognized the various currents of Marxist thought but argues that "to the extent that they remain fully Marxist . . . they are not compatible with the Christian concept of society" (8.8). One can only take "fully Marxist" to mean in line with official Marxism. The theologians alluded to in our first chapters and the method in theology they espouse can hardly be shown to belong to this school.

It may be true that there are examples of an uncritical employment of Marxist categories in some theological endeavors,[10] but the theologians under consideration in chapters 1 and 2 do not fall into this category. The Peruvian episcopacy has defended the orthodoxy of Gutiérrez, as did the late K. Rahner. Metz is in critical dialogue with the self-critical Western Marxism of the Frankfurt school, whose thoroughgoing critique of instrumental rationality was just as relevant to the former East bloc. As we have seen, Boff's critique of Western economic structures contains the same thrust. Segundo has devoted the greater part of a major work to demonstrating how eminently critical is his employment of Marxist concepts.

In reply to the original—non-magisterial—criticism, Boff takes issue with the contention that Marx is the founding father of liberation theology: "Here we need to speak clearly: liberation theology has always intended to use Marxism as a mediation, as an intellectual tool. This is the epistemological status of Marxism in liberation theology. In this manner, Marxism, inasmuch as it can, has some of its categories incorporated into the discourse of faith and not the contrary. Here it is theology that is in the position of metatheory and not Marxism."[11]

In critically employing certain aspects of Marxism as intellectual tools, our five theologians are in continuity with a long Christian tradition that is, in fact, an aspect of the inculturation of the gospel. This is the tradition of using the best available secular analysis of a given area of human experience in a creative, corrective, and surpassing way to make the faith more relevant under new circumstances. St. Thomas' use of Aristotle— a process also open to exaggeration and danger and for the magisterium of the time containing dubious aspects—is the classic example. Moreover, this approach to a qualified use of Marxist analysis follows on from a groundbreaking statement of John XXIII: "Neither can false philosophical teachings . . . be identified with historical movements that have economic, social, cultural or political ends, not even when these movements have originated from these teachings . . . and still draw inspiration from them. . . . Who can deny that these movements, insofar as they conform to the dictates of right reason and are the interpreters of the lawful aspirations of the human person, contain elements that are positive and deserving of approval?"[12]

Inasmuch as a theology from the perspective of the poor includes a social-analytical dimension, it implies the concept of a class option and therefore raises the question of class struggle. Our view of class struggle is that it is a syntactic rather than a prescriptive concept. It is an observation of what is the case rather than a prescription of what should be. Per se, it is a social reality demanding a Christian interpretation, just as the orthodox Marxists have given it their explanation. Marx himself never claimed "class struggle" as an original insight of his and made this clear: "As to myself, no credit is due to me for discovering the existence of classes in modern society and the struggle between them. . . . What I did that was new was to prove (i) that the existence of classes is bound up with particular historical phases in the development of production; (ii) that the class struggle necessarily leads to the dictatorship of the proletariat; (iii) that this dictatorship itself constitutes the transition . . . to a classless society."[13]

What is specifically Marxist is not the existence of class struggle but its interpretation in terms of the dictatorship of the proletariat. Even Lenin makes the same point: "Those who recognize only the class-struggle are not yet Marxists; they may be found not to have gone beyond the bounds of bourgeois reasoning and politics. To limit Marxism to the teaching of the class-struggle means to curtail Marxism. . . . A Marxist is one who extends the ac-

ceptance of the class-struggle to the acceptance of the dictatorship of the proletariat."[14]

What is more, class opposition as well as the awareness that
is built on it has been part of the magisterial teaching at least since
Pius XI. "Society today still remains in a strained and therefore
unstable and uncertain state because it is founded on classes with
divergent aims and hence opposed to each other and consequently
prone to enmity and strife."[15]

That the working-class vindicates its rights not simply through
the personal conversion of property owners but through struggle
is taught even more recently by John Paul II. "[Unions] are indeed a mouthpiece for the struggle for social justice. . . . This
struggle should be seen as a normal endeavor for the just good."[16]
In commenting on this, G. Baum[17] has spoken of "an imagina-
tive rethinking of class conflict" and of "the Christian Socialism" of John Paul II.

Class struggle is not a discovery of Marx but part of the structure of society, not to be ignored by Christians but to be interpreted in a manner consistent with the gospel. One step in such
an interpretation is the attempt to read the tradition consciously
from the standpoint of that class of people that is systematically
impoverished.[18]

Libertatis Conscientia

Our essentially positive appraisal of *Libertius nuntius* seems
justified by the tone and content of the second instruction on liberation, "for between the two documents there exists an organic
relationship. They are to be read in the light of each other."[19]

"Without claiming to be complete" (9)—an indication that the
debate is continuing—*Libertatis conscientia* set out to "highlight
the main elements of the Christian doctrine of freedom and liberation" (2). Stressing that the "aspiration to freedom has its first
source in the Christian heritage" (5), it critiques the "ideology
of progress" that followed from the Enlightenment (7). Despite
the political and social objectives of the modern liberation movement, it suggests that the fact that "new forms of servitude and
new terrors have arisen" points to "serious ambiguities concerning the very meaning of freedom" (10). Thus the contemporary
situation is one where "within nations and between nations, rela-

tionships of dependence have grown up which within the last twenty years have been the occasion for a new claim to liberation" (12).

The juxtaposition of the terms "dependence" and "liberation" in this sentence indicates an implied acceptance of the problematic of the liberation theologians. Thus, in its graphic description of new forms of oppression, it notes that "it is in the context of power relationships that there have appeared movements for the emancipation of young nations, especially the poor ones" (17). Because of history's frequent relapses into alienation and slavery, it concludes that the liberation movement remains ambiguous. Yet the instruction is clear about the priority of the liberation of the poor and equally of its theological roots, pointing out "a fact of fundamental theological and pastoral significance: it is the poor, the objects of God's special love who understand best . . . that the most radical liberation . . . is the liberation accomplished by the death and Resurrection of Christ" (22).

Outlining the tragedy of the perversion of man's freedom through sin as resulting in the self-defeating desire "to achieve fulfillment by himself and to be self-sufficient in his own immanence," the document, starting with the Exodus, moves to a consideration of Christian freedom. Immediately one notices a difference in nuance from its predecessor in that "the major and fundamental event of the Exodus . . . has a meaning which is both religious and political."[20] While the emphasis continues to be on spiritual poverty, nonetheless, in another important development of emphasis, the sinfulness of structural oppression is recognized. In the light of the gospel, "many laws and structures seem to bear the mark of sin and prolong its oppressive influence on society" (54).

Turning to the liberating mission of the Church, the document begins by stating that "the political and economic running of society is not a direct part of her mission" but that "divine love which is her life impels her to a true solidarity with everyone who suffers" (61). In promoting justice "she is not going beyond her mission." Likewise, "she exercises her judgment regarding political movements . . . which are contrary to the Gospel." Stressing that Christ "chose a state of poverty and deprivation," finding among the humble "hearts ready to receive him" and that he also wished to be near to those who, though rich, were marginalized, the document clearly points out that he chose "to be identified with the least of his brethren." Consequently, the document argues, "the special option for the poor, far from being a sign of particularism or sectarianism, manifests the universality of the Church's being and mission" (70).

With these statements the document may be said to have endorsed the position of CELAM at Medellín and Puebla in affirming the option for the poor, its Christological basis, and its structural dimensions as well as its preferential nature. From this standpoint the text then goes on to make a point of cardinal importance for the present task: "Similarly a theological reflection developed from a particular experience can constitute a very positive contribution inasmuch as it makes possible a highlighting of aspects of the word of God, the richness of which had not yet been fully grasped" (74).

Given the context of this illuminating development, which is a virtual paraphrase of a seminal statement of Gutiérrez, the phrase "a particular experience" can only mean the option for the poor.

Moving on to a consideration of the praxis of liberation, the text emphasizes that the Church's social teaching is born "of the encounter of the Gospel . . . with the problems emanating from the life of society." In adopting this organic approach, which leaves behind an exhortatory deductivism and resumes the program of *Octogesima adveniens,* the text appeals for subsidiarity and solidarity to the exclusion of both individualism and collectivism, paying attention once again to the question of structures and the need to analyze them. Structures "being necessary in themselves, often tend to become fixed and fossilized as mechanisms relatively independent of the human will, thereby paralyzing or distorting social development and causing injustice" (75).

The instruction stops short of granting "priority to structures and technical organization over the person," arguing that "it is therefore necessary to work simultaneously for the conversion of hearts and the improvement of structures." From here the text resumes the position of *Laborem exercens* on struggle and solidarity, stressing again the priority of labor over capital. The Marian conclusion centers on the Magnificat and sees in its interpretation a theological task "to help the faith of the poor to express itself more clearly and to be translated into life."

Concluding Remarks

Libertatis conscientia confirms our positive appraisal of *Libertius nuntius,* even if it falls somewhat short of enthusiastically endorsing a thoroughgoing liberation theology from the perspective of the poor. Nonetheless, it does mean that the theological project being outlined in the present work can, even in official terms, be included as a valid and acceptable Catholic theology.

Notes

[1] *Instruction on Certain Aspects of the "Theology of Liberation"* English trans., Vatican Polyglot Press (C.T.S. London, 1984). Original title *Libertius nuntius,* CDF, August 6, 1984. References to this document are given in the text.

[2] *Libertius nuntius* (hereafter LN), Introduction para.7. Cf. paras. 3, 6.

[3] LN, 8.2, 4, 7, 9. On the problematic nature of transcendent ethics for Marxist thought, see the fascinating article of Yuri Barabash, "What is Right?" *Literaturnaya Gazeta* (105) (Moscow, August 31, 1963). This is published in English together with many reactions in the Appendix to A. Solzhenitsyn *For the Good of the Cause* (London, 1971). On Christian ethics surpassing the historicism and utilitarianism of Marxist thought, cf. R. Belda, "Reflexión cristiana sobre la ética marxista." *Pentecostes* 16:52 (1978) 19-29.

[4] See the article in *30 Giorni* (March 1984), published in English as "From the Vatican, a Growing Concern," *Nath. Cath. Register,* August 5, 1984, as well as *Rapporto sulla Fede* (Milano, 1985). The difficulty is compounded by the fact that in these works J. Ratzinger is writing as a private individual, whereas LN comes from him in his official capacity. This distinction has also been recognized by John Paul II. Cf. "The Tablet" (September 14, 1985) 949. It leaves the theologian with the following question: What is the status of a statement in LN which is similar, if not identical, with one in RSF when the latter can be shown to be obviously a matter of opinion? Cf. also P. Hebblethwaite, *In the Vatican* (Oxford, 1987) 89, where Ratzinger himself is quoted as saying his views are "purely personal" and "do not commit the institution of the Holy See." *See also* C. Boff and L. Boff, "Convocotoria geral en prol da libertação (Carta aberta ao Cardeal Ratzinger)," REB 46 (1982) 251-262; and *New Blackfriars* (June 1985).

[5] J. L. Segundo, *Theology and the Church* (London, 1985) 27.

[6] Ibid., 34; LN 4.3; *Theology and the Church,* 47.

[7] Document of the Peruvian episcopacy on the theology of liberation (November 1984), published in English in OR (January 4, 1985) 5f. There is an enlightening commentary on this text by C. E. Gudorf in *Commonweal* (February 8, 1985) 77-79.

[8] On the various trends in Marxism as well as the critical movements within and between them, *see* L. Kolakowski, *Main Currents of Marxism* (Oxford, 1981). Cf. also D. McLellan, *Karl Marx: His Life and Thought* (London, 1983); and J. Merquior, *Western Marxism* (London, 1986) L. S. Feuer, ed., *Marx and Engels: Basic Writings* (New York, 1959). On ideology as false consciousness, cf. K. Marx, *The German Ideology in Feuer,* 245-260; D. McLellan, *K. Marx: His Life and Thought,* 89f. Cf. the statement of Cardinal Casaroli cited by Hebblethwaite, "In the Vatican," 71-72.

[9]Althusser dissents from the Eurocommunists' decision to drop "the dictatorship of the proletariat." In a manner open to serious questioning, Althusser locates an "epistemological break" in Marx's post-1845 work. After this we are dealing with the "real" Marx. Here the "true subject" of history is "the relations of production." In short, Althusser and his followers stress the traditional primacy of economic factors in Marxist theory to the extent of a sheer economism. He also reintroduces the concept of ideology in a functionalist sense, as a "social glue." Althusser's "orthodoxy" extended to defending Stalinism.

[10]Consider, e.g., "Red China and the Self-understanding of the Church" by the Theological Writing Collective (Filipino) in *Christianity and the New China* (Pasadena, 1976). It proceeds from an unnuanced and uncritical acceptance of "Marxism-Leninism —Mao-Tse-Tung Thought," abandoning reference to the magisterium (p. 130). One's "neighbor" is explicitly and exclusively identified with the "oppressed masses" (p. 132). This would be rightly dismissed as ideological reduction. Published in A. Kee, *The Scope of Political Theology* (London, 1978) 130–138.

[11]"Aqui precisamos falar claro: a Tdl sempre entendeu usar o marxismo como mediação, como ferramento intellectual, como instrumento de análise social. Eis ai o estado epistemológico do marxismo na Tdl. Desta sorte, o marxismo, no que podia, teve algumas de suas categorias incorporadas ao discurso da fé, e nao ao contrário. Aqui a teologia está na posição de meta-téoria e não o marxismo." L. and C. Boff, "O Grito da Pobreza á partir da Fé," *Folha de São Paulo* (March 24, 1984) 47 (English trans. ours). Cf. J. Ratzinger, "La teologia de la liberacion en debate" *Oiga de lima* (January 23, 1984); K. Fussel, "Ueber einige Aspecte des Marxismusverstandnisses der Kongregation fur die Glaubenslehre" in Venetz and Vorgrimler, eds. *Das Lehramt der Kirch und der Schrei der Armen* (Freiburg, Schweiz, 1985) 105–136.

[12]John XXIII, *Pacem in terris*, AAS 55 (1963) 257–303, n. 159.

[13]Letter to J. Wedemeyer, March 5, 1852. Cf. Marx-Engels *Werke* (Berlin, 1962) 28:507f.

[14]V. I. Lenin, *The State and Revolution* (1917) (New York, 1943) 30.

[15]Pius XI, *Quadragesimo anno*, AAS 23 (1931) 117–228, n. 82.

[16]John Paul II, *Laborem exercens*, n. 20. Cf. also nn. 8, 12.

[17]G. Baum, *The Priority of Labor*, Paulist (1982) 120. J. Joblin would argue that John Paul II remains a critic of socialism though having gone beyond it, as it were. "Jean-Paul II et les Socialismes," NRT 108:1 (1986) 47–63.

[18]Obviously, a complete critique of Marxism is beyond the scope of the present discussion. Here we are seeking to indicate (A) that Marxism is not unself-critical, and (B) that liberation theology does not employ it uncritically. Our fundamental argument here is that Marxism is not an omniexplicative *Weltanschauung*, and so unless one is to ignore it completely, it must be possible to make a workable distinction between a scientific use of certain analytical aspects (historical materialism) which are open to verification/falsification as in the case of any hypothetical analysis that does or does not achieve its intended task and, on the other hand, its classical claim— nonverifiable and certainly not verified in history—to be itself "the" science of reality (dialectical materialism). It is at this latter level that Marxism is unremittingly materialist and atheistic. Insofar as the Marxist view of religion is nonverifiable, it is based on a transcendent principle which would contradict Marxism's pretension to being materialist. Inasmuch as the Marxist view on religion claims to be "scientific," it has not been verified and is therefore mistaken. Moreover, Marx's view of religion, fragmentary and undeveloped, contradicts his own view of superstructure. On the nonverification and nonverifiability of Marx's view of religion, cf. A. van den Beld, "Karl Marx

en het einde Van de Religie," *Nederlands Theologisch Tijdschrift* 30:1 (1976) 37–54. Needless to remark, the positive approach to dialogue with Marxism implicit in our approach should not obscure the evangelical imperative in its regard. Cf. R. Coste, "Témoigner de Jésus Christ devant les Marxistes," NRT 111:2 (1979) 161–192.

[19]Congregation for the Doctrine of the Faith, *Instruction on Christian Freedom and Liberation,* March 22, 1986. English trans., Vatican Polyglot Press (CTS London, 1986). The original title is *Libertatis consientia,* hereafter LC. Cf. LC 2. References to this instruction are given in the text.

[20]Compare LC 44 with LN 4.3.

5

The Dimensions of the
Option for the Poor

The aim of this chapter is to indicate what is involved in the option for the poor for the theologian. Right away a clarification is called for. In our consideration of local theologies, we saw that the Christian community at the local level is not only the recipient but also the subject of theology. Insofar as such a community is composed of poor people seeking to transform the conditions of their marginalization in the light of the gospel, there is already an option for the poor in a very direct way. Here, however, we have in mind what may be termed the academic theologian, one who has been formed in the tradition and who exercises an intellectual service in the understanding of the faith.

Preliminary Understanding of the Option for the Poor

A preliminary understanding of the option for the poor is to see it as the personal orientation of theologians. They will share this orientation partly in function of belonging to a particular tradition within "the Tradition," formed by their background, experiences, and conversation partners, and partly in function of personal decisions consequent on their self-appropriation as intellectuals, as moral human beings, and as disciples of Christ. To approach theological method on the basis of the theologian's own self-appropriation seems justified by the post-Englightenment turn to the subject as exemplified in the transcendental methods developed by Lonergan and Rahner.

The option for the poor may be justified in principle as the practical base of a theological method on the basis of the origin of the Judeo-Christian tradition in the Exodus narrative of liberation; the focusing of this tradition in the religion of prophetic monotheism with its denunciation of greed and marginalization; the fulfillment of this tradition in Jesus, who demonstrates a preferential concern for the marginalized and who on the cross is the poor and marginalized person par excellence; the constant motif in the history of the Church of the importance of the turn toward the poor in the moral teaching of the Fathers;[1] the rise of the Mendicant and Vincentian movements; the growing radicalization of the social teaching of the magisterium; and the present-day pastoral concerns of the people of God. It is also a notable theme in the ministry of John Paul II.[2]

Further Clarification

A further clarification may be outlined as follows. The conscious operations of the theologian occur at several levels, corresponding to the multidimensional phenomenon that is the thinking-acting person. The interpenetration and mutual enrichment of the following four dimensions offer a relatively adequate description of the contextualization of any intellectual undertaking, including theology:

1. The individual-personal dimension: The theologian as a person is a unique human individual with her own incommunicable self. She has her call; she makes her options; she follows her convictions.

2. The interpersonal dimension: The theologian as a human person appropriates himself and becomes himself only in relation to others. This is partly a matter of personal history and partly of choice. Coconstitutive of his being a person and of his orientations are those with whom he spends his time, those with whom he communicates in seeking to express *koinōnia,* those with whom dialogue is no mere occasional academic exercise but his daily bread. Those with whom he speaks will inevitably bear a close resemblance to those for whom he believes he speaks.[3]

3. The structural dimension: Every human being is a social agent, and it is impossible to discourse on social reality without sociological imagination. The very existence of sociology as a

science implies the inaccessibility of the shape and details of social reality on a purely common-sense basis. The illusion that the
shape and significance of social reality are simply a matter of "taking a good look" generally obscures the fact that our view is
predetermined by the conventional wisdom operating in function
of the dominant ideology. Any theology that seeks to discourse
critically and systematically on a social reality similarly requires
a socioanalytical hermeneutical mediation. Every theology, implicitly or explicitly, employs such mediation. A theology seeking to make an option for the poor will employ that analytical
model whose underlying values are consistent with the gospel and
which explicitly privileges the aspirations and the optic of the poor.

4. The institutional dimension: Every human being and any theologian belongs to an institution or set of institutions. In the theologian's case, these will be a university, a Church, a religious
order, not to mention the many secular institutions of which he
is part—sometimes barely consciously. In its operation every institution is ambiguous. But normally, in the depths of its own
vision and inspirational basis, it possesses the capacity for self-
correction and renewal. In the case of the Church, this is classically expressed by *Ecclesia semper reformanda*—thus implying
the existence of a *reformandum*. The theologian shapes his institutions but equally is shaped by them, sharing their ambiguities
and ready to challenge them and be challenged by them.

Option for the Poor: Its Four Dimensions

As applied to the option for the poor, these four dimensions
may be defined as (A) evangelical simplicity, (B) existential solidarity, (C) transformational analysis, and (D) institutional challenge.

We shall now attempt to spell out what is meant by each of
these as well as to indicate their necessity, limits, and intercon-
nections.

Evangelical Simplicity

To make the option for the poor one must become poor: not
in the sense of an absolute misery, which would result in a total
ineffectiveness at the academic level, but in the classic sense of

detachment from wealth and privilege proposed by the Gospels, the Christian tradition, and, in particular, by the religious life. It is primordially a personal belief in and personal witness to the radical dependence of all living things upon the beneficence of God. As such, it sets its face against a mere formalism in this regard, for evangelical simplicity sees the difference between discoursing upon our absolute dependence on God and living with such security that we do not really depend upon him at all.

This option contains a prophetic element inasmuch as it is a countersign to the prevailing ethos of selfishness. It seeks to be a visible statement that theology is a faith-based scientific enterprise in the service of a world of fraternity and human dignity, without which God's design to create human beings in the image of his Triune life is frustrated. By the same token, it seeks to unmask the greed that lies behind the comfort and pseudo-culture of the privileged.

The theologian seeking to embrace evangelical simplicity is an intellectual who is refusing the role of providing a legitimation mechanism for the status quo. He is no longer naive about the relationships between wealth, power, culture, and schooling. He realizes how science and learning can be domesticated and chooses instead to put his science at the service of a kingdom that is not of the spirit of this world.

Such a theologian has become aware of how easily the intellectual can internalize the achievement orientation of contemporary Western culture, especially for one who has status and qualifications. Evangelical simplicity creates conditions for the rediscovery of the gospel vision of time, money, and talents: to see them as the possibility of creative and fraternal service to and solidarity with those who suffer. The theologian distances himself from a chronic individualism that runs counter to the fundamentally communitarian thrust of the gospel and promotes a privatized emphasis on career and promotion, as evidenced by the manner in which both theology and spirituality are in danger of becoming just two more marketable products for the willing consumer. In the Western Church, where so many theologians are celibates, this takes on an added dimension. For celibacy is an intensification of the evangelical imperative of disponibility for universal love as a sign of the eschatological kingdom. Thus, it is a radicalization of evangelical simplicity. As such, evangelical simplicity is an ontic moment in the process of conversion of the intellectual who is also a Christian.

If such a personal orientation is prophetic as countersign, it is also prophetic as an anticipatory gesture indicative of a human future for all men and women. Such a future—itself an anticipation of the kingdom of God—is only possible on the basis of a new discovery of the possibility and need for simplicity in those parts of the world that enjoy an excess of material benefits, usually at the expense and on the backs of the suffering of others. The theologian as an articulator of the faith of the Church has a particular calling in reminding the Church of what it believes and of what it is called to be: the servant and the sacrament of a renewed humanity that gives thanks to God. In our times, this will consist principally in the Church facilitating by example the emergence of a new quality of human solidarity possible only on the basis of simplicity of life-style.

Existential Solidarity

As one who seeks to articulate a faith addressed to all men and women but in a special way to those who are poor, the theologian herself seeks a living *koinonia* in the faith with people who are poor and oppressed. Realizing that as a human being she becomes herself through relationality with others, she faces the question of who these others may be. She may wish to be *omnibus omnia* but is likely to realize that this can be effected only at the level of spiritual solidarity and intentionality. Her human finitude demands that she stay with the power of the particular and that she live with and for all through living intensely and loyally with and for a few.

The self-critical theologian is aware that her investigating, reflecting, understanding, and judging remain partially formed by the confinements of culture, social class, and superego. Unknown to herself, what she articulates can be the unconscious echo of the preoccupations of privatized religion in a bourgeois world. It sometimes requires a genuine intellectual conversion for the theologian to realize that the world of the academy, seminary, or university is not the world of the poor and suffering. It can require a quantum leap of imagination and grace for it to come home to her that her conversation partners are for the most part the intelligent, the articulate, and the privileged and that she has never in reality heard the voice or the cry of the poor.

For it is crucial for the theologian to grasp the conditions under which she can speak for or about the poor. For the world of the oppressed, unlike the academy, is a "culture of silence" where people have never been allowed to speak for themselves; where they have deeply internalized the prejudice that would mark them off as inferior. To speak for the poor is first of all to speak with them; to speak with them is to create conditions under which they can speak for themselves.

It is here above all that the dialogical nature of the Christian's presence to the other for mutual enrichment in the truth must be given its full weight. The theologian must be freed by a profound act of humility for the realization that she can and must learn from the poor. For the poor, open to God from the "the underside of history," have a particular experience of God, which not only complements hers and acts as a corrective to overvaluing it, but is in principle more primordial and privileged, since the marginalized are the primary recipients of the gospel.

Consequently, the theologian is present to the poor first as a learner. Seeking to read the book of their experience requires genuine solidarity. There can be no theology that is not a reflection on ecclesial faith; there can be no ecclesial faith without *koinōnia;* there can be no *koinōnia* that does not privilege solidarity with the poor. Only an ecclesial situation that exists in function of the rights of the poor to express and celebrate their experience provides the basic material for Christian theological reflection, because anything less leaves out not merely one element of the Church but its most significant one.

Transformational Analysis

The need for sociological analysis, implying the inaccessibility of the shape and details of social reality on a purely common-sense basis, also discloses the naiveté and inadequacy of a merely individual or interpersonal approach to the question of poverty and the poor.

Traditional Christian doctrines such as solidarity in sin and in redemption, the mystical body, and the representative nature of worship and prayer all imply a view of reality that cannot be limited to the individual and interpersonal dimensions. In a postindustrial situation where the concept of class, even though not exhaustive, is essential, the option for the poor implies an option for a social group or class and its perspective and aspirations. Two qualifications are necessary here. The first follows from the nature of the local social reality. The second follows from what we believe to be an important distinction between the classical Marxist and Christian understanding of the poor.[4]

In a Third World country it is scarcely an oversimplification to identify the "poor" and the "people," for it is often the vast majority of the population that is silenced and marginalized. In a First World situation the poor can often be a marginalized minority, usually very heterogenous with little common identity[5] and quite distinct from the employed working class, who by comparison can appear quite settled. While the former can often be dismissed by the orthodox Marxist as the *Lumpenproletariat,* with no revolutionary potential, for Christianity it is they who are the privileged ones. It is for this class that the Christian makes a preferential option, maintaining "strategic links" with leaders and groups of the "progressive class," for otherwise the marginalized remain detached from the possibility of initiating structural change from the perspective of their own aspirations.

To deal theologically with this complex reality requires an interdisciplinary approach. Here theology requires a necessary socioanalytical hermeneutical mediation to deal with sociopolitical reality, just as it would require a psychological hermeneutical mediation to deal with the details of the dynamics of personal spiritual growth. In both cases, of course, theology will deal with the results of such mediations according to the science of theology, that is, specifically in the light of faith seeking understanding, but the actual material for reflection will be furnished by the analysis. The operation and the operator are theological, but the *operatum* is sociological. Theology deals with the absolute and with the absolute significance of the concrete but possesses no absolute language with which to do so. Even for theologians, "correct ideas do not fall from the sky."

Clodovis Boff has confronted the principal epistemological obstacles to this approach.[6] He presents them as follows:

1. Empiricism: In this view there is a direct and immediate contact with the real, presuming a zero degree of objectivity whereby "the facts can speak for themselves."

2. The illusion of common sense: Common sense, inasmuch as it tends to operate at the level of undifferentiated consciousness, is inevitably an expression of the prevailing ideology and the acceptable fashion.

3. Methodological purism: This is the denial of interdisciplinarity, or the opinion that theology does not need the results of other disciplines. It is the methodological analogue of *sola fides* at the doctrinal level and overlooks the fact that theology is constructed with human materials drawn from human cultures.

4. Theologism: This is a variant on the preceding point and holds that only theology can give an adequate account of the real. This view, the methodological analogue of supernaturalism, ignores sociological imagination and the autonomy and interdependence of the sciences.

5. Semantic mixing and bilingualism: What Clodovis Boff means by these is, in the first case, the borrowing of terms but not method from socioanalytical mediation without integration into the theological method. The second is a synoptic use of both sociological and theological language without clarification. In both cases, two parallel universes of discourse merge without integration. Eventually one triumphs over the other to the detriment of both.

This brings us to the conclusion that any attempt to theologize about a given social reality, including the perspective of the poor, requires socioanalytical hermeneutic mediation. Consequently, there is a constitutive relationship between such a mediation and the theological interpretation of the reality under investigation. This is far more than a relationship of application, which sees the former as essentially extrinsic to the latter, emphasizes a duality of autonomy, and sees social analysis as a purely technical exercise. Here we are speaking of an organic interchange between the two, where the analysis really is part of the theological interpretation to which it is referred. This allows us to see both the methodological basis as well as the implications of an important statement of Paul VI: "It is up to Christian communities to analyze with objectivity the situation which is proper to their own country, to shed on it the light of the Gospel's unalterable words

and to draw principles of reflection, norms of judgment and direc-
tives for action from the teaching of the Church.''[7]

The question now becomes the choice of model: Having demonstrated the constitutive importance of social analysis, on what basis shall one choose the analytical model?

At a general level, an analytical approach may be distinguished
from merely descriptive-functional approaches.[8] Among the
former, three clear tendencies may be further distinguished:

1. What may be termed the traditional model, which views reality as cyclical and repetitive and, in an authoritarian way, views
change and conflict as deviant. Implicitly, this model operates
from the "top down" and privileges the perspective of the
powerful.

2. What may be termed the liberal model, which is an evolu-
tionist or progressivist view of reality that seeks to modify change
through a balance of forces and managerial technique. It seeks
to adjust change rather than either prevent or promote it.

3. What may be termed the transformational model, which is
the one being adopted in the present work. Explicitly embracing
a transformational view of reality, it seeks to operate on the basis of widespread participation and promotes a creative understanding of change and conflict on the basis of privileging the
perspective of the poor.

None of these models is value free, for there is no interest-free
knowledge. The set of values enshrined in identifiable applications of any of these models may not in particular cases match
those of the gospel. But faith provides the fundamental ethical
thrust, on the basis of which we choose analytical models, efficacy
structures, and ideologies. Neither the Gospels nor the social
teaching of the Church espouses particular models but, rather,
the values on the basis of which they may be chosen. It is the interpenetration and interdependency of these two levels that are
precisely at issue here. "A values-structure which ignores the complex problem of its effective realization will end up serving different values. An efficacy structure which forgets the values it is
serving and gets carried away by its presumed autonomy will lose
the achievement-orientated efficacy it exhibited at the start."[9] Because of the "eschatological proviso," the most the theologian
can demand is the critical theological employment of the analyti-

cal model whose underlying practical values structure is least in disaccord with the gospel.

As already indicated, our choice is for the transformational model. Evangelically, this choice is based on the belief that the gospel is more primordially a power for renewal and transformation than for order or management. Ethically, it is based on the grounds that it explicitly favors the perspective of the poor. Epistemologically, it follows from the unity of knowledge and emancipative interest.[10] Pastorally, it follows from the present trends in ministry and mission. Methodologically, it is the socioanalytical model organically linked to the development of a theology that takes the option for the poor as its hermeneutical perspective.

This approach would appear to find support in both the methodology and content of the Medellín and Puebla documents. Methodologically, what is involved is a process paralleled, at least in principle, by the Greek Fathers' use of Plato, Aquinas' employment of Aristotle, and Rahner's reading of Heidegger. The secular scientific hypothesis best adapted to the reality about which one wishes to theologize is chosen—with discretion and not without qualification—to give a preliminary reading, which is then reread in the light of the word of God.

Institutional Challenge

The theologian operates within an institution or set of institutions not only for effectiveness but in principle. All institutions share the morally ambiguous character of the human condition—the quality of being *simul justus et peccator*.

The principles of structural and social analysis must also be applied to the seminary, the university, the publishing house, the religious order, and the Church itself.[11] Any serious interpretation of the doctrine that we are a Church of sinners cannot rule out a priori the possibility that in a given historical situation, the institutions to which the theologian belongs can, in a significant measure, be allied to structures of power and privilege that do not always operate in the interests of genuine emancipation of the poor.

Even as the theologian seeks to investigate and uncover a need for institutional self-criticism, he is merely applying to theology's concrete context the social teaching of the Church. This concrete theological context does not merely transmit this teaching but is itself challenged by it. He has only to read the organic development of this social teaching,[12] from *Rerum novarum* to *Laborem exercens*. There he finds an initial outrage at what is happening to working people, together with a clear enunciation of their rights. This develops into a condemnation of both totalitarian extremes and the mapping out of a third way. In time, what is being expressed is an overt commitment to the process of socialization in the world of work and capital, together with an openness to the enrichment of this process by ideas coming from hitherto questionable sources. A powerful identification with the people of our times in all their struggles and aspiration is then given a new urgency in the context of world poverty. A further development comes in the introduction of the inductive-analytical approach to the question, thereby moving beyond primarily didactic and exhortatory approaches.[13] The development continues as he reads that the struggle for justice is a constitutive part of the preaching of the gospel and that salvation is the integral liberation of the whole human person. The teaching then moves on to explicitly proposing the priority of labor over capital as well as the right of the workers not just to ask for but to struggle for what is rightfully theirs. Finally, he will hear—as a Christian—the invitation to make a preferential option for the poor. As a theologian he is called to expand and clarify this and by the same token to allow his own methodological perspective to be expanded and clarified in turn.

The same dialectic of challenge and reform can be seen in the contemporary developing awareness of the understanding of poverty in religious life. Authentic religious life, following from the impulse of the Spirit, represents a true *locus theologicus*. It is, in a derived though still specific way, a locus of God's action and self-revelation. The renewal of the constitutions of many religious congregations in relation to the meaning of evangelical poverty represents a synopsis of much of what we are saying in this chapter. In various examples of such renewed constitutions one notes the inclusion of the structural dimension of poverty; the call to live in actual solidarity with the poor; a refusal to allow the realities of poverty and the poor to be spiritualized of all socioeconomic content; the need for an inductive analytic approach in apostolic undertakings; the creative retrieval of the spirit of the founder in the light of contemporary theological method; and an insistence that the study of theology is itself in the service of the poor.

This results in new models of holiness.[14] Traditional models are seen in their historical context, and their supposed normative significance is reinterpreted. There is a call for an incarnated holiness, for an engaged spirituality, and for political saints.

That these directions are not simply correctives to an imperturbable tradition in need of minor adjustments, much less passing fads, can be seen from a glance at the demographic shifts within world Christianity. Already a majority of the world's Christians live in the "South." This will shortly be true of Catholicism too, with a clear majority in Latin America. De facto, Catholicism will in any event become the religion of the poor, a process that may be accelerated by the decline in religious practice in the "North," as materialism and the privatization of religion take their toll.

The Necessity, Limits, and Interconnectedness of the Four Dimensions

Without evangelical simplicity, there is no personal engagement of the theologian in acquiring the perspective of the poor. It is one thing to grasp the "concept" of the option for the poor, which may then become another chapter in theological *Ideengeschichte,* but that is something other than making that option.

Without existential solidarity with the poor and oppressed, the theologian operates as a traditional rather than as an organic intellectual and cannot articulate their experience. His distinct task of articulating in a systematic way what was articulated with more primordial experience but with less differentiated consciousness is fundamentally dependent upon a genuinely dialogical relationship with the poor.

Without a transformational analysis of society, the option remains at best naive and at worst blatantly ideological, in the sense of actually justifying by default the situation of marginalization, by refusing to unmask its structural causes.

Without a dialectical relationship to his institutional context, the theologian risks either being adrift or simply reinforcing unconscious structures of privilege or disconnectedness. He can neither invite the academy to examine its own structural role in society nor test the intellectual rigor of his own conclusions.

Evangelical simplicity alone is detached and ineffective. Combined with existential solidarity it becomes concrete and engaged but remains naive without integrating into itself a transformational analysis. Solidarity without simplicity is paternalistic, as simplicity without solidarity is disconnected. Analysis alone is academically removed from real persons and their pain and joy: with solidarity, it takes on life; with simplicity, it opens itself up to conversion. The institutional alone degenerates into narcissistic consolidation. With solidarity, it takes on flesh and blood; with simplicity, it becomes credible; with transformational analysis, it becomes real.

Concluding Remarks

Our concern in this chapter has been to present the option for the poor as a matrix of four mutually interpenetrating dimensions. Where each theologian or team of theologians will be situated in this matrix will, in practice, be a matter of discernment calling for both courage and realism: courage, inasmuch as it calls for a departure from the predictable and the commonly accepted; realism, for if one is to remain a theologian one cannot lose sight of the fact that the perspective of one's work, the hermeneutical standpoint from which it proceeds, is not yet the work itself and still demands the scholarship and intellectual rigor of the academic. The hermeneutical standpoint does not per se guarantee this rigor; it merely makes it possible.

This understanding of the option for the poor includes the liberation perspective but goes beyond it. Likewise, it both includes and subsumes the perspectives of personal simplicity, lived solidarity, and institutional critique. It seeks to be holistic, corresponding to the four essential dimensions of human being and acting in the world.

We have sought to give here essentially a description of what this hermeneutical perspective entails. This description makes several methodological assumptions—about the social rootedness of thought, about praxis, about cognitive interest, and about hermeneutical theory. It remains to establish these methodological foundations more securely, and it is to that task that we now direct our efforts.

Notes

[1] On the virtually forgotten patristic teaching on this matter, *see* C. Avila, *Ownership: Early Christian Tradition* (New York, 1983); W. Schewring, *Rich and Poor in Christian Tradition* (London, 1951); J. de Santa Ana, *Good News to the Poor: The Challenge of the Poor in the History of the Church* (New York, 1979).

[2] *See* especially his address to the Brazilian episcopate, where he said, "Vos sabeis que a opção preferential pelos pobres, vivamente proclamada por Puebla . . . é uma convite a uma solidariedade especial com os pequenos e os fracos, os que suffram e choram, os que são humilhados e deixados a margem da vida e da sociedade. . . ." OR (July 12, 1980) 2. In his address at the Favella of Vidigal he noted that "a Igreja em terra Brasileira quer ser a Igreja dos pobres," OR (July 4, 1980) 1. In his Christmas address to the Roman Curia in 1984 John Paul wrote, "I would like to mention . . . the 'preferential option for the poor.' . . . This 'option' stressed so strongly by the episcopate of Latin America to-day has been repeatedly confirmed by me, following the example of my unforgettable predecessor Pope Paul VI. I gladly take this opportunity to repeat that this commitment to the poor constitutes a dominant theme of my pastoral activity. . . . I have made and continue to make this 'option' my own. I identify with it. . . . It is my option . . . which is unwavering and irrevocable." "The Charism of Peter at the Service of Unity," RfR 44:3 (1985) 321-330.

[3] The option for the poor demands an unequivocal "conversion to the people." "The man who proclaims devotion to the cause of liberation, yet is unable to enter into communion with the people . . . is grievously self-deceived. . . . Conversion to the people requires a profound rebirth. Those who would undergo it must take on a new form of existence; they can no longer remain as they were." P. Freire, *Pedagogy of the Oppressed* (London, 1967) 37. This can not be achieved from "outside": it is an aspect of the inculturation of the theologian that can aptly be termed "class suicide." Theologians, through their education belong to a different class from the poor, thus there is a temptation to paternalism in their outreach. Cf. A. A. de Melo, "Classe media e opção pelos pobres," REB 170:43 (1983) 340-350. The theme of middle-class intellectual among the oppressed is explored in great detail by Freire. For a popularized presentation *see* Irmão Michel, "Communidades catolicas de base são o fruto de collaboração entre duas classes sociais, a pobre e a meia," REB 165:42 (1982) 120-127.

[4] It seems to us that there is an important distinction between the Marxist and Christian understanding of poverty and the poor. The classical Marxist *Verlendungstheorie* merely changes the parameters of the problem by privileging the "progressive" class rather than the "least of the brethren." Cf. K. Blaser, "Christliches und marxistiches Verstaendnis der 'Armen,' " ZfM 6:4 (1980) 199-212; W. Post, "A Christian Critique of Marxist Solutions for the Problem of Poverty," Con 104 (1972) 73-79. By contrast the late Marxist philosopher J. Lukacs essays a sympathetic Marxist evaluation of the Christian approach in "The Problem of Poverty and the Poor in Catholic Social Teaching," Con 109 (1977) 62-71.

[5] Summarizing the conclusions to their study on poverty and social policy in Ireland, L. Joyce and A. McCashin note that "since the poor form a heterogenous and differentiated mass, it is difficult for the poor themselves to develop a common identity

and a common organization to represent their interests at national level." *Poverty and Social Policy* (Dublin, 1982) 112. In terms of popular movements for transformation, one must clearly distinguish the "marginalized" of the "First World" from the "people" of the "Third World." Cf. also C. Boff, *The Way Forward for the First World Church,* CIIR (London, 1986).

⁶*Teologia e Prática,* 67f.

⁷Paul VI, *Octogesima adveniens,* AAS 63 (1971) 401–441, n. 4.

⁸J. Holland and P. Henriot, *Social Analysis* (Washington, 1980). This relatively modest book has had an enormous impact; cf. Orbis ed. (1983) ix. On models of social analysis, *see* 31–34.

⁹Segundo, *Faith and Ideologies,* 177; cf. 129–130, 257–260, 266.

¹⁰Cf. ch. 6.

¹¹The divine institution of the Church as well as its infallible extraordinary magisterium and its indefectibility do not necessarily guarantee a total lack of moral ambiguity in its institutions. Y. Congar remarks, "On ne peut pas attribuer un acte moral comme tel à une collectivité. Mais on peut lui attribuer des fautes, des manquements, des incompréhensions, des médiocrites," *Sainte Eglise* (Paris, 1963) 143. For a postconciliar opinion on the question, *see* K. Rahner, "The Sinful Church in the Documents of Vatican II," TI, 6, esp. p. 277. Cf. also ch. 10. Prior to present developments in theological method, J. Alfaro noted how Catholic theology lacked the sort of criticism of religious institutions derivable from a sociology of religious institutions. "Téologia, Filosofía y Ciencias Humanas," Greg 55 (1974) 209–238.

¹²The term "organic tradition" is used in this context by D. Dorr, *Option for the Poor: A Hundred Years of Vatican Social Teaching* (Dublin, 1983) 252.

¹³On the significance of this development, cf. M. D. Chenu, *La Doctrine Sociale de l'Eglise comme Idéologie* (Paris, 1979) 87–90. He sums up these developments in "The Church's Social Doctrine," Con 171:1 (1984).

¹⁴Cf. F. Urbina "Models of Priestly Holiness: A Biographical Review," Con 129:9 (1979) 88–98. Note the comparison of priestly holiness inherited from the *"Ecole Française"* with that rooted in emancipative praxis.

6

Securing the
Methodological Foundations

The purpose of this present chapter is to explore further the principal methodological assumptions of a theology developed from the optic of the oppressed. Such a theology derives its impetus from the contemporary situation of chronic poverty, inequality, and oppression. It sees in this situation not only a subject for theological exploration—as in the manner of a simply genitive theology—but also an actual horizon of theologizing. This, in turn, means that theology is articulated not simply as a "perennial theology" from which one makes deductions but rather, in function of and from the standpoint of an involvement in the pressing issues of the day. It is the consequent capacity to ever articulate the Word anew that makes theology perennial.

In the second place, it seeks to argue that conversion to the optic of the poor is not only an exigency of Christian action in the world but is, in fact, a condition of the possibility of theology.

Third, theology from the perspective of the poor clearly locates itself among those theological methods that would subscribe to the primacy of praxis. The primacy of praxis, of course, does not per se establish the hermeneutical privilege of the perspective of the poor; still, establishing the former is a methodological requirement for discussing the latter.

The fourth methodological requirement of the theology under discussion here is its assumption that the theological task does not halt upon completion of its literary-critical and historical-critical hermeneutical functions. Theology from the side of the poor is not simply a retrieval of the tradition in the light of the new hermeneutical question, but a theology that is self-critical both in respect of hermeneutics and of the tradition, though still in continuity with it. At base, it is a theological position informed not simply with an interest in explication and conceptual clarity but, more profoundly, with an interest in emancipation. A theology operating from the optic of the poor is therefore a theology with an explicitly acknowledged and articulated engagement: it does not wish to be neutral, and it denies that theology can ever be neutral. The methodological basis of such an approach may be found in demonstrating how a cognitive interest in emancipation informs the whole of critical reflection, allowing scientific endeavors to go beyond positivism and the illusion of value-free investigation. A theology guided by this interest can surpass the limitations of a purely technical deductivism or a solely explanatory hermeneutical function and retrieve its true identity as the knowledge of God born out of and elaborated for the sake of human emancipation and redemption. To this end we must first investigate how critical reflection is informed by a cognitive interest in emancipation.

In the fifth place, we must investigate the sociopolitical origin and destination of all theology. Theology that privileges the optic of the poor makes no pretense at being sociopolitically neutral. But in adopting this stance, it argues that all theological investigation is sociopolitically rooted, even if unconsciously so.

Thus, in order to establish epistemically the legitimacy, necessity, and validity of the option for the oppressed as a hermeneutical principle of theology, this chapter will seek to show the following:

1. How theology today must remain organically linked to the poverty issue, the massive catastrophic suffering of whole peoples.

2. How conversion to Christ present in the poor is constitutive of the reality that the theologian is, and thus of all theological reflection.

3. How theology is governed by a redemptive-emancipative cognitive interest that goes beyond a solely explanatory function.

Following this, in our next chapter we will continue this line of inquiry in order to show the following:

4. How theological theory is always grounded in praxis.

5. How all theology has a sociopolitical rootedness and destination.

Theology and the Poor:
The Contemporary Issue, the Contemporary Context

If "the joys and the hopes, the griefs and the anxieties of the people of this age" are also those of the "followers of Christ," then the principal issue for contemporary theology is surely the horrendous specter of world poverty and oppression. We are, of course, assuming here that salvation comes to us in and through the consummation of the historical process, and that since God in Christ is incarnate, drawing all of creation and history to himself, theology is always a theology of history and of the world. For the community of the followers of Christ "realizes that it is truly and intimately linked with humankind and its history."[1]

Poverty, however, is not just an issue for theological reflection in a genitive sense. There can be, of course, a theology of poverty in this sense whereby—quite legitimately and not without purpose—the theological data as presently understood are applied to the phenomenon of poverty with a view to deducing certain exigencies of Christian praxis. But that is only half the story, because theology is not just a matter of dealing with the great issues that confront humankind on its journey toward salvation from the perspective of a previously established horizon and in terms of a finally developed body of doctrine. It is just as fundamentally, if not more so, a matter of expanding that horizon and developing that doctrine from the perspective of a vitally engaged involvement in such an issue. For one does not just read the present; one also reads with the present.

This is an entirely biblical approach. Creation, Exodus, covenant, Exile, restoration, wisdom, prophecy, and apocalyptic are never solely issues or phases in Israel's history dealt with by the inspired authors in a merely doctrinal way out of an already established and self-contained theological tradition. Rather, it is out of the horizon of these experiences that tradition itself is established. Unlike the Enlightenment, Israel's question was not, Is there a God? but What kind of God? The Exodus was partly understood with reference to a preconception of what God was like, but more profoundly the Exodus provided the horizon from which it was possible to move to a more adequate notion of God. More profoundly still, when we speak of Jesus revealing God, we hardly mean that Jesus plays out a role corresponding to God's supposed attributes. We mean rather that the life, death, and resurrection of Jesus actually disclose to us what God is really like. Therefore it is the praxis of *sequela Christi* and not just the concepts in the New Testament that forms the horizon from which to think about God!

Revelation is comprehended in relation to the whole of history, and it occurs as event in history. The reception of this revelation, which occurs not primarily as word but as event, is the creative reception on the part of active, living subjects. The recipients of a text always become cocreators of its meaning. Scripture does not yield its meaning entirely by itself. It requires tradition, which is the active presence of revelation in living subjects, by the power of the Holy Spirit.[2] The tradition—because it is living—is never finally articulated but is permanently retrieved and enriched through being interpreted on the basis of new experience. Because it is God's word, it is always more than equal to these new questions, "yielding riches old and new." The theologian, then, is one who is organically linked to both the tradition and the great issues of contemporary experience. She or he does not simply explain the latter in terms of the former but also seeks to retrieve the former—in a creative and faithful reformulation—from the horizon of the latter. This retrieval is always an interpretation because all understanding is interpretative.

What we are seeking to indicate here is simply this: the theological tradition, if it is to be theological, that is, the knowledge of the God who saves, and if it is to be part of the tradition, that is, the active presence of revelation in living subjects, cannot ignore the great contemporary issues of poverty and oppression. But it does not simply study these phenomena: it is itself retrieved and deepened as a consequence of being "received" by subjects active in the process of making a Christian response to this situation. As well as being an object of theological investigation, involvement in the struggle of the poor becomes a horizon of theological understanding. A theological interest in the poor and oppressed necessarily implies an interpretation of theology from the perspective of the poor. It indicates a theological method whose hermeneutical standpoint is an option for the rights of the oppressed.

Conversion to the Poor as
Constitutive of Theological Perspective

For the classical theologian, the suggested turn to the "option for the poor" as a privileged hermeneutical perspective may involve a change in mentality, in socioethical stance, and even in his notion of God. In other words, it involves intellectual, moral, and religious conversion.

In this section we shall seek to demonstrate that this threefold conversion is foundationally constitutive of a truly theological perspective to the extent of it being a condition of its possibility and, as a consequence, that conversion to Christ in the poor, constitutively realized as conversion to the optic of the poor is, in the case of a strictly Christian theology, fundamental to Christian moral and religious conversion. In this way, we shall seek to argue that conversion to the perspective of the poor is constitutive of a Christian theological perspective.

Toward the conclusion of his *opus magnum, Insight,* which "may be construed as a remote contribution to the method of theology," Lonergan resumes a great part of his considerations by urging the reader to come to the mind of Aquinas, not by learning off his conclusions within some putative Thomistic system, but by "appropriating his own rational self-consciousness." In its own way a statement of the primacy of praxis, this approach points to the importance of theologians being thinkers who attempt to grasp "the dynamic structure of their own cognitional and moral being."[3]

In applying this to method in any science, which for Lonergan is "a systematic pattern of recurrent and related operations yielding cumulative and progressive results," he aims not simply at rules but at normative patterns from which rules may be derived. His underlying assumption is that quite distinct from and even prior to any concept are the transcendental notions that constitute the very dynamism of our conscious intending. For Lonergan, this dynamism is not the product of any scientific achievement but, rather, the condition of its possibility. He argues that this transcendental method has several functions, to which each of his "functional specialties" correspond. It is not a new method; it is simply the explicitation of a process already there. It is, however, only part of theological method; it supplies the basic anthropological component. It does not supply the specifically religious component.

What we wish to investigate here, following Lonergan, is the intellectual, moral, and religious conversion that is the condition of "being in love with God"; and then to see whether and how this is foundational for theological method. Of specific interest here is Lonergan's fifth functional specialty: foundations. This is quite different from traditional fundamental theology inasmuch as it presents "not doctrines, but the horizons within which the meanings of doctrines can be apprehended"; in other words, the possibility of a hermeneutical perspective. "Foundations" emerges through the thematization of the notion of conversion: "As conversion is basic to Christian living so the objectification of conversion provides theology with its foundation." This conversion, "as lived, affects all of a man's conscious and intentional operations. It directs his gaze, pervades his imagination, releases the symbols that penetrate to the depth of his psyche."[4]

Of particular significance for present considerations is Lonergan's insistence that conversion is also historical: a movement with its own cultural, institutional, and doctrinal dimensions. Foundations thus goes beyond the role of dialectics, which aims only at clarifying issues; it demands a "fully conscious decision about one's horizon, one's outlook, one's world-view. It deliberately seeks a framework in which doctrines have their meaning. . . . Such a deliberate decision is anything but arbitrary. . . . It is a total surrender to the demands of the human spirit: be intelligent, be responsible, be reasonable, be in love."[5]

Here he clearly sees beyond the individual and cognitive dimensions of praxis. M. Lamb[6] sees Lonergan as one who "critically responds to the concerns of the dialectical and materialist phase of the turn towards the subject." The experiment in "generalized empirical method"—the term that was to become Lonergan's preferred description of his method—is conducted by the historical process itself: "Conversion is more than a change of horizon. It can mean that one begins to belong to a different social group. . . . It would be efficacious in the measure that the group is dedicated not to its own interests but to the welfare of mankind." And this "threefold conversion is not a set of propositions that a theologian utters but a fundamental and momentous change in the human reality that the theologian is."[7]

For Lonergan, intellectual conversion is the radical clarification and elimination of misleading assumptions concerning reality. Moral conversion is the process of allowing the criterion of one's decisions and actions to change from satisfactions to values. It involves the capacity to opt for the truly good even when value and satisfaction clash. Religious conversion is being in love "without restriction" and as such is "the efficacious ground of all self-transcendence."

As regards the relationship of mutual interdependence, "it is possible when all three occur within a single consciousness to conceive their relation in terms of sublation. . . . What sublates goes beyond what is sublated and introduces something new and distinct . . . preserves all its proper features and properties and carries them forward to a fuller realization within a richer context."[8]

Just as moral conversion procures the pursuit of truth—which is the task of the thinker on the path of intellectual conversion—by arming the thinker against bias, so this religious conversion through "being in love without restriction" provides a new basis in all valuing and doing good.

Consequently, religious conversion is foundational to theological method and is constitutive of its cognitive process to the point of being a necessary condition of its possibility. For Christians, conversion to Christ present in the least of his brethren is always constitutive of religious conversion. A conversion to genuinely dialogical *koinōnia* with the least of Christ's brethren would, therefore, change the horizon of the theologian's thinking and change even the reality that she or he is. This change and the hermeneutical perspective following from it is thus foundational to the theological method of a strictly Christian theology.

The Redemptive-Emancipative Interest of Theology

Sciences are distinguished not primarily with regard to the object of their inquiries but rather with regard to the horizon of their inquiries.[9] There is a science of theology because of the existence of the Absolute in its quality of self-communicating redemptive love. Inquiring into the nature of reality from this perspective yields a particular kind of information, which is intimately related to possibilities of action of a certain sort, just as the acquisition of this perspective is itself related to the same possibilities of action. Theological perspective is impossible for one who wishes to live superficially—the acquisition of a religious vocabulary notwithstanding. The Absolute in its reality as self-communicating love is known not merely as an object of contemplation but as making possible redeemed existence, as expressed in the living of a new quality of human solidarity, by which living humankind is truly in the image and likeness of the Blessed Trinity.

Theology is, in this sense, the science of the Absolute. But it does not possess an absolute language, nor any pattern of conceptualization that is outside or above history. Theology can hardly wish to be less incarnate than the Eternal Word himself. As such, it seeks to articulate possibilities of being and action in the world that do justice to the dimensions of authentic humanness revealed in the paschal mystery and the gift of the Holy Spirit. Now, this science of theology has an underlying interest, because the horizon of understanding that makes it to be theology—and not for example, philosophy or the sociology of religion—is grounded in certain possibilities of action and produces a body of knowledge intimately related to these possibilities of action.

The cognitive interest of theology is related to a matrix of meaning whose principal elements may be communicated by terms such as redemption, holiness, *koinōnia,* reconciliation, liberation, worship, justice, and peace. One could simply say "God," but God is always God-for-us; his word is eternally *Verbum incarnandum,* and thus theology is always (theological) anthropology. The being and action proposed by these and other congruent terms point to a new quality of human solidarity, the existential expression of the kingdom of God present "already and not yet." The meaning of a given class of scientific statements is intimately related to certain possibilities of action, and the meaning of the class of scientific statements proper to theological science is intrinsically related to the possibilities of being and action indicated here. Theological science is rooted in and directed toward a dimension of human being and action that is the historical reflection and repercussion of the outpouring of the Holy Spirit and that makes possible a new quality of human solidarity. The perspective of the poor is, we argue, privileged in seeing how this solidarity may come about. Such a theological method, which privileges the perspective of the poor, operates very explicitly out of a clearly defined interest and even claims that theology itself must share this interest as a condition of its possibility. Thus the question of the cognitive interests of sciences is of paramount importance. Following J. Habermas,[10] we shall attempt to spell out this epistemological perspective with a view to indicating its applicability to theology in general and, in particular, to the theological hermeneutic under discussion.

Emancipative Cognitive Interest

Habermas' approach to epistemology is an attempted retrieval of a critical theory whose starting point is an unmasking of positivism as a disavowal of self-reflection that conceals a commitment to technological rationality behind a facade of value freedom. He sees in contemporary technocratic consciousness a "negative utopia of technical control over history."[11] His theory of cognitive interests is in essence an attempt to radicalize epistemology by unearthing the roots of knowledge in life. He sees in the emergence of instrumental rationality the universalization of a technical interest in the prediction and control of objectified processes in the natural environment. This, he holds, is rooted in an "anthropologically deep-rooted interest," which he calls "technical interest."

The historical-hermeneutical sciences are rooted in another "anthropologically deep-seated interest": in securing and expounding the possibilities of self-understanding in an intercommunicative life based on consensus. He terms this "practical interest." The critical-reflective sciences are rooted in an "emancipatory interest," aimed at freeing people from pseudonatural constraints on their humanness: "These cognitive interests are of significance neither for the psychology nor for the sociology of knowledge, nor for the critique of ideology . . . for they are invariant . . . not influences on cognition that have to be eliminated for the sake of objectivity of knowledge: rather they themselves determine the aspect under which reality can be objectified and thus made accessible to experience in the first place, they are . . . the necessary conditions for the possibility of experience which can claim to be objective."[12]

In this sense of "invariant," Habermas holds that these *Erkenntnisinteressen* have a quasi-transcendental status.[13] His point is that prior to the orientations influenced by sociological and psychological factors, different types of theoretical statements are in different reference frames corresponding to different fields of exigency of human action.

As a consequence of their rootedness in specifically different structures of human action and reflection, they will also employ a different logic of inquiry. Habermas points out that "there is a systematic relationship between the logical structure of a science and the pragmatic structure of the possible applications of the information generated within its framework."[14]

Thus, in order for theology to be capable of generating insights whose practical repercussions will be agapeistic and redemptive, the structure of theology as a science must be informed by a horizon of investigation governed by a redemptive cognitive interest.

Basic to grasping the "emancipative interest" of critical theory is the insight that reason itself has an interest in emancipation.[15] Habermas argues that this general correlation between knowledge and human interest can only be grasped by correlating the emancipatory interest behind critical theory with self-reflection. Reason's own meaning and autonomy imply an interest of reason that is constitutive of knowledge as such. Reason does not provide its own foundation but derives from the self-constitution of the human species. For Habermas, reason, in self-reflection, becomes congruent with emancipative interest.

The interest of self-reflection in emancipation can, then, as soon as it takes into account the social structures of reality, be viewed as an interest in social relations organized on the basis of a communication free from domination. Correlatively, knowledge produced in an inquiry directed by emancipative interest assumes a therapeutic role in relation to the systematically distorted communication that arises because institutionalized power-relations are legitimated and then rooted in such distorted communication between ideologically imprisoned consciousnesses.

To see the implications of this analysis for theology, we begin by noting theology possesses less its own language as much as its own way of employing language—and thereby, its own vocabulary. Theological conclusions are reached neither by angelic intuition nor by common sense: they are the fruit of two processes of hermeneutical mediation, the first making experience intelligible, the second transforming this level of intelligibility to that of theological truth.

The conclusions operated on by the processes of theological reasoning are intermediate conclusions reached through a scientific process whose underlying quasi-transcendental interest is one of emancipation. Already to that extent, theology includes this emancipative interest. In the theological *Aufhebung,* it not only exercises its emancipative interest but intensifies it. For just as freedom in Christ is an intensification and elevation of human emancipation, so the *Erkentnisinteresse* of theology is an incorporation and intensification of the emancipative interest of the critical sciences.

In this argument, we are attempting to establish the applicability of the concept of emancipative interest to theology. Of course, just as the sciences can succumb to the imperialism of technocracy and the instrumentalization of reason, so, too, can theology. What Rahner castigated as *Denzingertheologie* is a form of theological positivism. For here, too, theology has come to mean a logically integrated system of conclusions in lawlike dependence on hermetically sealed assumptions. Theology, here, is not cognitive praxis but pure technique, requiring not insight but formulae. Equally, theology can operate out of an essentially practical interest resulting in a form of functionalism. Communication occurs, but the psychosocial rootedness of the discourse is never examined.

However, since the logical structure of a science is systematically related to the action that can follow from the information it generates, theology, as the knowledge of God-who-redeems-us, operates with a redemptive cognitive interest. The truths that it generates are not conceptual adornments but truths for our salvation, which is integral liberation. This redemptive cognitive interest incorporates the emancipative interest of critical theory. The critical interest is thus incorporated into theology's logical structure, so that its hermeneutical perspective consciously incorporates an interest in an egalitarian, communitarian life-praxis free from distorted communication. Given the privilege of the poor in the Christian tradition as the primary architects of *koinōnia,* such a redemptive-emancipative hermeneutical perspective would be constitutively achieved by proceeding from their standpoint.

Concluding Remarks

Three of the methodological assumptions of a theological method rooted in the struggle of the poor—an organic linkage to that struggle, a conversion to the optic of the poor through a genuine communion with them, and a demonstration of the redemptive-emancipative cognitive interest of theology—have been explored in this chapter. By seeking to demonstrate that these methodological parameters apply to theological science in general, we have attempted to indicate the validity of the hermeneutical perspective under investigation. We must now conclude this part of our investigation by exploring the primacy of praxis in theological reflection as well as theology's sociopolitical rootedness and destination.

Notes

[1] On the development of an ecclesiology of immersion in history, *see* C. Moeller's commentary on the "Preface and Introductory Statement of *Gaudium et spes*" in H. Vorgrimler, ed., *Commentary on the Documents of Vatican II*, 5 vols. (London, 1969) 5:77–114.

[2] Y. Congar, *The Tradition and The Traditions*, 401f. Cf. also 253f.

[3] *Insight: A Study in Human Understanding* (London, 1957) 739f., 748: "It is only through a personal appropriation of one's own rational self-consciousness that one can hope to reach the mind of Aquinas. . . . " Id. *Method in Theology* (London, 1972) xii.

[4] *Method in Theology*, 131.

[5] Ibid., 268.

[6] M. Lamb, in *Creativity and Method: Praxis and Generalized Empirical Method* (Milwaukee, 1981) writes, "If Lonergan's early work can be seen as transposing the basic presuppositions of the transcendental-idealist phase, then I believe his later work (from *Method in Theology* to his present work on macroeconomics) can be viewed as a creative and critical response to the challenge of the dialectical-materialist phase of the turn towards the subject." *Creativity and Method*, 61.

L. J. O'Donovan makes a not dissimilar point in relation to Rahner in "The legacy of K. Rahner's last years," TS 46:4 (1985) 621–646. "Rahner's later thought sought an increasingly temporal and historical conception of God and the people of God."

This understanding of praxis in the thought of Lonergan is something many of his commentators have not recognized. Cf., e.g., F. Kerr, "B. Lonergan's Method," NB 57 (1976) 117; C. Davis, "Lonergan's appropriation of the concept of praxis," NB 62 (1981) 114. Both see his work in solely individualist terms.

[7] *Method in Theology*, 269, 270.

[8] Lonergan specifies that he means sublation in the sense used by Rahner. Cf. *Method in Theology*, 241.

[9]Thomas Aquinas, ST 1, q. 1, a. 1, r2. "Diversa ratio cognoscibilis diversitatem scientiarum inducit."

[10]J. Habermas, *Erkenntnis und Interesse* (Frankfort, 1963); English trans., *Knowledge and Human Interests* (Boston, 1971). *See also* T. McCarthy, *The Critical Theory of J. Habermas* (Cambridge, Mass., 1978) 53–125. Apart from the several references to Habermas in *Analogical Imagination,* cf. also E. Schillebeeckx, *The Understanding of Faith* (London, 1974) 124–155; T. Groome, *Christian Religious Education* (San Francisco, 1980) 172f., 182; and J. Kroger, "Prophetic-Critical and Practical-Strategic Tasks of Theology," TS 46 (1985) 3–20.

[11]J. Habermas, *Theory and Practice* (London, 1974) 276.

[12]*Knowledge and Human Interests,* 311.

[13]This terminology is somewhat problematic. It is not a question of going "back to Kant." Since, as Habermas claims, these cognitive interests have their basis in the natural history of the species, "the human interests . . . derive both from nature and the cultural break with nature." *Knowledge and Human Interests,* 312–313.

[14]*Theory and Practice,* 8–9.

[15]*Knowledge and Human Interests,* 287. Clearly Habermas has introduced a hierarchy of interests, but on what basis? P. Ricoeur, in "Ethics and Culture: Habermas and Gadamer in Dialogue," PT 17 (1973) 153–165, writes that "the explicit epistemological function seems to be derived from an implicit axiological position, similar to the one which led Max Scheler to place the person at the summit and heart of his ethics," p. 162. Our theological incorporation of Habermas is not therefore a reduction of theological method to the method of critical social theory because his epistemology itself implies an ethical option that in turn is rooted in a transcendent values structure.

7

The Primacy of Praxis
and the Sociopolitical Rootedness
of All Theology

The Primacy of Praxis

In discussing the problem of the theory-praxis relation in theology, it is important to keep three levels of the discussion distinct. First, that of Christian living: of faith, hope, and love as a daily lived reality. Second, that of theology, which grows out of and reflects back on this first level. Third, that of a critical reflection upon the method of this systematic reflection. Each of these levels is in some sense theological, though in a different way. Insofar as no faith statement is capable of articulation in an entirely pretheological way, the articulation of Christian praxis—even the very employment of the term "Christian"—is always a theological statement, however rudimentary. The second level, classically defined as *fides quaerens intellectum,* or as we might phrase it, *amor preferentialis pauperum quaerens intellectum,* is that of a differentiated theological consciousness. The third is a hermeneutical or metatheological level, a systematic reflection on systematic reflection. It is relatively straightforward to cite a clear primacy at the first and third levels: praxis at the first, theory at the third, though the theory-praxis dialectic remains operative. At the first level it is essentially a matter of what we do, and at the third level, even an attempt to understand and articulate the primacy of praxis in theology—such as we are now attempting—would itself be a theoretical task.

It is at the second level that debate arises. Each of the theologians enumerated in our first chapter, exemplifying a theology as elaborated from the perspective of the poor, argues for the primacy of praxis in theology. Implicit in our own exposition of the dimensions of the option for the poor is an argument for the practical basis and goal of all theological reflection. Thus, arguing a hermeneutical privilege for the perspective of the poor in theological reflection is making a statement about the primacy of praxis in theology. It is not that the primacy of praxis per se necessarily establishes the privileged status of this perspective. The praxis whose primacy is either argued or established could remain at a purely individual and cognitive level. It could also be a pragmatism uncritically articulated. Thus, a theological method granting a hermeneutical privilege to the optic of the poor assumes the primacy of praxis over theory in theology, though in a nuanced way.

English is fortunate in distinguishing "praxis" from "practice." The conscious choice of the term "praxis" may be seen as an attempt to retrieve the Aristotelian distinction between *praxis* and *poiésis*[1] in a post-Modern situation marked by the imperialism of technocracy. By praxis we mean—as a first approximation—doing, considered as reflective, purposeful, self-critical human performance, as distinct from mere making. Praxis is governed and informed by "prudence" *(phronésis)* whereas *poiésis* is what is involved in the application of technique *(techné)*. As a first approximation to the meaning of theory, we mean that process of self-critical purposeful reflection that is intrinsic to praxis and that, when adequately concluded, makes it possible to say that something is true and real. It is through theory that the active subject, committed more primordially to reality through praxis, grasps objectivity. But it is through praxis that he or she becomes a subject. One can see on this reading why theory can never sublate praxis while praxis can and does sublate theory.[2]

These preliminary approximate definitions of praxis and theory are necessary but still probably insufficient to make the terms—as they appear in the theologians—univocal. Shades of meaning derive in principle from the reflex character of the relationship between them, which changes according to the historical development in the meaning of the terms.[3]

From the time of Pythagoras, *theoria* has connoted contemplation of the eternal. The Neoplatonists distinguished it from knowledge *(epistemé)* as immediate apprehension from discursive cognition. In Aristotle—the greatest influence before the Modern period—the eternal, unchanging, and necessary is known by theory or theoretical knowledge *(epistemé theoretiké),* and this alone is considered to be knowledge in the true sense precisely because, being knowledge of what is necessary, it can be exact. Human action and the human good are known by practical reason *(epistemé praktiké),* which, because it seeks insight into connections that are by nature contingent, requires "prudence" *(phronésis)* and is, in principle, inexact. What is makable through the application of *techné* is known by *epistemé poietiké,* which may be termed "technical reason."

Because of the achievement of St. Thomas, who essentially transposes the Aristotelian notions of theory and praxis, and the neo-Thomists, this Aristotelian notion of theory and praxis and, by implication, of the primacy of theory over praxis, has continued to heavily influence theology. Yet the supposed grasp of that which is eternal, unchanging, and can govern reality through teleological necessity can forget that all language and all conceptuality—since there is no nonlinguistic thinking—spring from our dealing with the world and with entities within the world, for there is no such thing as a point outside history from which the identity of a problem can be conceived. The cost of such an approach is to risk canonizing as perennial what is, in reality, an extrapolation from what is contingent and is therefore historically conditioned and dependent. What is invariant is method, not theory.[4]

The problem of the theory-praxis relation changed as soon as what was regarded as theoretical knowledge became relevant to the shaping of the world, especially as a result of the scientific revolution. The post-Cartesian situation laid the foundations for the present-day imperialism of technocracy by the loss of the *praxis-poiésis* distinction, leading to the view of action as manufacture. The Cartesian split resulted in the supplanting of *praxis* by *techné.* Theory came to mean a system of propositions built up in a strictly deductive fashion, its premises considered to have the self-evidence of axioms. This approach held a vicelike grip upon scientific thinking until the revolution in twentieth-century physics. By a strange irony, a parallel kind of positivism can be

found in the method—if not in the basis—of much nineteenth-
and pre-Vatican II twentieth-century theology, especially in what
has been aptly termed *Denzigertheologie*.

The heritage of the Enlightenment is twofold in this regard.
Insofar as theory can enlighten one's understanding of reality by
uncovering what are regarded as sociopolitical restraints, then theory is itself a form of social practice. The Kantian dichotomy between a phenomenal order, which can be theoretically discerned,
and a numinal order, which can only be postulated, bequeathed
a divorce between theory and practice. With Hegel the emphasis
shifts to praxis as a social activity, but in a manner that left itself
open to the Marxist critique of seeking to change the world by
seeking to change our idea of the world. In the *Theses on Feuerbach,* praxis is argued to be the achievement that constitutes man
and the world of his experience. This leaves praxis determining
theory—in the orthodox Leninist interpretation nondialectically—
though this could hardly explain the originality of Marx's own
thought. When, in Soviet ideology, this understanding of Marxist praxis became the sole criterion of truth, the result was a be-
haviorism of the left with praxis once again reduced to *techné*.

In the neo-Marxism of the Frankfurt school, the development
has been different. A critique of the prevailing reductionist view
has led to a retrieval of the Aristotelian contention that a theory
of praxis is fundamentally inconceivable, leading to a renewed
dialectical approach to the theory-praxis relation. J. Habermas
is the inheritor of this tradition and has emerged as the most vehement critic of the contemporary technocracy and scientism and
especially of its pretense to a purely disinterested theoretical interest in knowledge. In this view, theory has degenerated into a
solely technical interest, and all hermeneutical and critical thinking is thereby reduced to technique.

The Theory-Praxis Dialectic in Theology

These various shades of meaning of both theory and praxis account in large measure for the wide variety in the meanings of
these terms as well as the different ways in which the reflex character of the relation between them is couched, often implicitly, by
the theologians. M. Lamb has sought to thematize various models

of the theory-praxis relation in contemporary theology. He enumerates five:

> The primacy of theory type maintains that religion and theory are intrinsically related while both have only an extrinsic relation to praxis. The primacy of praxis type envisions that religion and praxis are intrinsically related while theory remains more or less extrinsic. The primacy of faith-love type insists that genuine Christianity is only extrinsically related to theory and praxis; is always non-identical with them. The final two types seek to sublate both the relational primacy models by developing what I term a both/and stance of critical correlation. Thus the critical theoretical correlation type emphasizes the theoretic mediation between Christianity and the categories of theory-praxis. The critical-praxis correlation type seeks to articulate a praxis- grounded mediation.[5]

Guided by this schema, let us attempt to see the relative status that might be accorded to a theology consciously articulated from the optic of the poor.

In the first type, no particular hermeneutical privilege can be assigned, since the view of the theory-praxis relation is entirely dependent on the Aristotelian position of the primacy of theory. In neo-Thomistic neoorthodoxy, the reflex character of the theory-praxis relation disappears. The emphasis is on the innate ability to know necessary truths, and theology risks becoming a deductivism. Practical theology, including any theology that concerns itself with the experience of the poor, is merely the application of what is deduced. Even in the attempted retrieval of this approach by J. Maritain, the acceptance of the Aristotelian notion of necessity always implies "a descent to action." Love for the poor and charity in any form would possess a merely cathartic or preparatory significance. Since praxis can in no way change the ontological structure of reality—the eternal and the necessary being the normative—privileging the perspective of the poor in theological method would be seen as an error, distracting the theologian from the pursuit of metaphysical theological wisdom.

The second type of relation is seen by Lamb as articulating an intrinsic relation between Christianity and praxis, with theory as an extrinsic reflection on that praxis. To see how a theology from the perspective of the poor as described in this work would be evaluated first demands distinguishing the various kinds of praxis that modern theologies have sought to privilege. Cultural historical activity with its Enlightenment rejection of metaphysics tends to identify the reign of God with human purposefulness, usually expressed in terms of historical secularity. As Metz, above all, has argued, this approach has consciously or unconsciously enthroned the concerns of the bourgeois subject in theology. Far from privileging the perspective of the poor, it ignores it, when it does not despise it. In a similar way, for example, in the earlier writings of H. Cox, an urbane political normativity for theology is suggested. The resulting pragmatism leaves little enough space for the optic of the poor. A more extreme notion of praxis is evident in the critical Catholicism of van Oudenrijn, Xhaufflaire, and Dergson.[6] In their view, only a theology that submits to the normativity of Marxist praxis could be authentically Modern. Prescinding from the question of the various interpretations of Marxist praxis, this approach, insofar as it would lead us to see all theology past and present as "bad theology," would appear to cut off any theological enterprise from its roots in the theological tradition: a rupture not only ecclesiologically undesirable but also hermeneutically impossible. No one, least of all a theologian, can leap over history and tradition. Moreover, a theological submission to Marxist praxis, in this particular sense, might not result in privileging the perspective of the poor but, rather, the perspective of the party.[7] The preferential option might not be for those who suffer most and for a view of God's coming reign from the point of view of their suffering but, rather, for that social grouping whom the party, for whatever tactical reason, considered to be in the vanguard of the revolution.

Lamb sees the third type of faith-love primacy as emphasizing a nonidentity of Christianity vis-à-vis theory and praxis, examples being the classic position of Barth or, more recently, that of Von Balthasar.[8] Theory-praxis retains no normative function for truth. These writers are not unconcerned with praxis nor, by implication, with the poor, but the touchstones of truth lie in "God alone." There is a lingering supernaturalism about the whole approach, which, while rightly emphasizing sanctity, makes enormous assumptions about what sanctity might be.

The critical theoretical correlation can be seen in the work of Bultmann, Rahner, Pannenberg, and Tillich, to mention four of its most outstanding exponents. As well as a concern to articulate the theoretical issues confronting theology in the post-Modern world, these writers tend to see the relation (unity in difference) between theory-praxis and theology as elaborated in an ontology doing justice to both history and transcendence. In the case of Rahner, the most notable example within that tendency, a transcendental anthropology seeks to ground a critical correlation between the ontological structure of human being-in-the-world and the exigencies of revelation. For Bultmann, the tool is Heideggerian ontology, correlated with human authenticity achieved through an act of faith-decision. Pannenberg seeks to correlate a universal historical perspective with considerations of the resurrection as a prolepsis of the end of history. The key, and ultimately, normative function for these theologies is a concept: faith-decision for Bultmann; ultimate concern for Tillich; absolute openness to absolute mystery for Rahner; anticipation of the whole of history for Pannenberg; retrieval of the classic in a new classic for Tracy. It could be demonstrated—easily in the case of Rahner—that none of these theologians is indifferent to the perspective of the poor, yet in each case normativity for the theological position is ultimately determined by theory. The perspective of the poor cannot, under these methodological conditions, be assigned any particular privilege, since these approaches, while not denying the reflex nature of theory-praxis, through identification with theory nonetheless give theory the first and final word.

The fifth type differs from the foregoing inasmuch as praxis is considered not only to be the aim of theory but also its very basis. Theory is grounded in praxis, that is, in purposeful self-critical human action. No theory qua theory can be critically self-grounded. No theory can be self-grounded,[9] and no praxis can be based upon a practical reason that is innocently free of self-criticism (as in the second type above). The theologians whose work we studied in our first two chapters as well as the model of theologizing outlined in chapter 5 all fall into this category. Thus the model of theology being proposed here differs from the first type by refusing to allow classical metaphysics, much less its descendants, to present itself as omniexplicative. It differs from the second type in demanding a self-critical rootedness in the tradition. It differs from the third type in demanding a normativity—even though not identity—for Christianity in theory-praxis. It differs from the fourth type by grounding theological theory in praxis.

Fundamental to this approach is the conviction that authentic praxis can never be understood by theory qua theory. In the work of Lonergan[10] we see a particularly enlightening example of the primacy of praxis. There is first a shift from theory to method. Within this method, meaning comes through meaningful self-appropriation. Philosophy-theology becomes an emancipative therapy. Theology elaborated from the perspective of the poor assumes the primacy of praxis as elaborated in this fifth of Lamb's five models. But if, as we see here, theology is always emancipative for the theologian and the community, then the question has to be asked, Can theology—strictly so-called—ever be undertaken except in critical collaboration with those who most demand emancipation? Insofar as freedom consists in living out what Lonergan termed the transcendental imperative, then theological praxis can never be separated from the struggle for emancipation, and the requisites of that struggle are most evident from the perspective of the oppressed.

The Primacy of Praxis in Theology

In what way are we to conceive of praxis as sublating theory? First, praxis is not activism: it is not immediate and direct external action. To say what praxis is, is already an act of reflection requiring theory.[11] There can hardly be a discussion of theory-praxis that, although it requires correct cognitive praxis, will not, within this dialectical relationship, result in a theory. Theory is thus intrinsic to praxis. It is, in fact, what gives praxis its strictly human character of reflective action as distinct from mere behavior. Praxis, therefore, always includes theory. Within the theological praxis, this theoretical moment has its own relative autonomy, and its rigor is to be judged on its own terms. If theory does prevent praxis from degenerating into pragmatism, the primacy of praxis prevents theology from believing it has changed the world through grasping the concept of change. Science is not reality but just one expression of it. No theory can have the competence to unify the totality of a given reality: that is the task of historical praxis. The primacy of praxis[12] is not ethical but analytic, exercising a causality not mechanical but dialectical. Praxis is the primary and material condition for theory, creating a space within which theory operates. Within this dialectical circle, theory intervenes in praxis to give it its specifically human character, which is the essence of praxis. In this way, there is praxis only in and through theory. The primacy of praxis does not diminish the demand for theoretical rigor; it deepens it.

The view that theological theory is grounded in praxis is fundamental to the thesis being argued here. Arguing that the perspective of the poor offers theology a hermeneutical privilege implies rooting and destining theology in the experience of the poor, and, methodologically, this depends on the primacy of praxis.

The Sociopolitical Rootedness and Destination of All Theology

A theology from the perspective of the poor assumes a privileged hermeneutical standpoint for a theological reflection emerging from the experience of the poor and destined to elucidate the ongoing theological conversation in terms of the image of God and his revelation that is attained by adopting this hermeneutic. Methodologically, this is a particular example or application of a more general principle, which involves seeing the implications of sociological imagination. For, without reducing theology to the sociology of theology, sociological imagination indicates that theological reflection necessarily proceeds from and returns to some sociopolitical rootedness that is, in principle, discernible. While this does not limit the scope of theology, nor deprive it of its proper formal object, it does imply that the one who would theologize can only do so from within a location in space-time that cannot be wholly abstracted from its sociopolitical foundations and implications. This characterization of theology is not particular to the project at hand but is intrinsic to any theological reflection.

Every theologian is also a member of a given society. She or he is a social agent. Theological reflection is not the fruit of a disembodied thought process employing ahistorical concepts or using an iconic language as if its terminology were not surrounded by circles of meaning that are historically rooted. All human thought and meaning is sociohistorically rooted, just as all understanding is a linguistic achievement with roots in human praxis. The significance and meaning of any and every theological achievement is necessarily endowed with a given social existence and codetermination. Although theology properly discourses on God, who is both absolute and ineffable—and "God" is no mere conceptual limit-concept in its discourse, for because of the incarnational nature of revelation, theology truly succeeds in discoursing on God—it does so by means of the *analogia fidei:* theological language is not itself either absolute or ineffable. Thus the option for the poor is simply one concrete example of a determinative parameter that is intrinsic to theology as to any human reflection.

We seek, however, to go beyond the position of merely stating, however passionately, that the perspective of the option for the poor is spontaneously demanded by the specter of massive poverty in the contemporary world. While such an approach, frequently employed by liberation theologians, is certainly ethically defensible, in the context of the present discussion, which is one of theological method rather than pastoral theology, it might leave itself open to the charge of theoretical pragmatism. It is one thing to state something; it is another thing to establish it! Belief is not the same thing as theoretical rigor. All we have established so far is that since all theology has a sociopolitical rootedness and determination, it always involves—implicitly or explicitly a sociopolitical option, the option for the poor being one such option. On this analysis the question for the theologian is not whether or not she or he is engaged but how and on whose side.

Many of those attentive to the specific nature and task of theology hesitate to see the distinction between "good" and "bad" theology primarily on the basis of its motivating interest. A theologian who is also a theoretician of the faith will point to the fact that from the point of view of the theoretical rigor of theological science, such a qualification is more an external differentiation than an internal explication. There is more to an intellectual discipline than its social significance. The fact that a given theological enterprise is elaborated from a demonstrably important sociopolitical perspective—for example that of the poor—is not per se a guarantee of its theoretical consistency. Equally, the fact that a theology may be correctly termed bourgeois might not prevent it from being in its internal core relevant and good theology.[13] What is involved here is the question of distinguishing and relating two levels of theological reflection corresponding respectively to epistemology and the sociology of ideas. At the latter level it is quite clear that the sociopolitical rootedness and destination of the given theological enterprise emerges in the theological production. At the former level, however, that of epistemology, it is more difficult to determine that the social rootedness of the theology conditions its epistemological rigor.

Following M. de Certeau, C. Boff has employed the notion of *permission* in this regard.[14] According to this view, a given political engagement would make possible a corresponding theological discourse. It would not, however, produce ipso facto the corresponding theological causality of relationship between the "sociopolitical cause" and the "theological result." Between them there remains a *rupture epistemologique*. Yet the two can never be separated, since they are dealing with one and the same subject and one and the same material object. The subject is one and the same; the material object is the same: namely, effective action from the standpoint of the poor; the formal object is different: on the one hand, theoretical rigor, on the other, social emancipation. De facto, the choice of thematic is always made in function of some explicit or implicit sense of sociopolitical rootedness and engagement, for theoretical reflection cannot be furnished except in and from a practical position. Everyone is standing somewhere.[15]

Thus the option for the poor, as with any decisive option, makes possible a different kind of theology. In doing so, it does not necessarily guarantee the theoretical rigor of the theology produced. Yet a decisive sociopolitical engagement is a necessary condition for theological theory itself to choose its theoretical object.

For some, the greatest difficulty in accepting this approach stems from a proper commitment to upholding the methodological gratuity and disinterestedness of a scientific inquiry. The only "interest" this approach would admit is an immanent interest in the methodological rigor of the scientific process itself. Yet no scientific process, however rigorous, no immanent, cognitive process, is ever neutral—or innocent! It always serves its interests. The sociology of ideas indicates that knowledge is always a form of power. The control—and worse still, manipulation—of knowledge in various political systems does not correspond to the invention of "knowledge as power." It is rather the abuse and distortion of the relationship that always existed. Because all knowledge is socially situated and politically orientated, however remotely at first sight, the choice of questions for research is determined, at least implicitly, in function of interests whose worth or otherwise cannot be guaranteed by the theoretical rigor of the cognitive process employed in their scientific investigation.

Therefore, just as the scientific value of a given theological project cannot be established on the basis of the sociopolitical option, neither can the question of political complicity be avoided by appealing to a putative scientific neutrality. This may be illustrated by reference to that most rigorous of theological theoreticians, St. Thomas. He set out to construct a scientifically exact and theoretically rigorous theological system on the basis of disinterested speculation. The inherent consistency and epistemological rigor of his method is without parallel. Yet, to speak in contemporary terms, it is impossible that the resultant scholastic edifice did not exercise an ideological role. In contemporary language, it operated as a legitimation mechanism for the ideals of a moral feudal order. While Aquinas was never an unself-critical ideologue for the status quo, his *Weltanschauung,* his questions, and the destination of his results were co-determined by "the existing order." His theology was not neutral; it was feudal. The standpoint that is beyond any standpoint is a pure illusion.

A Theoretically Rigorous Proposal

Our aim in these last two chapters was to attempt to demonstrate that the underlying methodological assumptions of the theological project being proposed in this work are in fact proper to theological science in general. Proposing the option for the poor as a hermeneutical perspective implies a fusing of horizons between involvement with the poor and reading the tradition; it implies the primacy of praxis; it implies conversion to the poor; it implies the principle that theology incorporate an emancipative interest; and it implies that theology is necessarily sociopolitically rooted and destined. For the perspective of the option for the poor to have more than a partial or local significance, it is necessary that these five qualifications apply to theology as such. That is what we have attempted to demonstrate, and in doing so, to establish the necessity and validity of a theology from the side of the poor. We now proceed to the heart of the matter: to establish the relative normative status of this theological perspective.

Notes

[1]Aristotle, *Nicomachean Ethics,* trans and ed. W. D. Ross, *Great Books of the Western World* (Oxford, 1952) 9:339f. Cf. also p. 388 c:2 and 389 c:1.

[2]*Method in Theology,* 292. "Genuine objectivity is the fruit of authentic subjectivity. It is to be attained only by attaining authentic subjectivity." Lonergan wishes to transcend naive realism where there is an apparent objectivity of immediacy. Objectivity is attained through meaning and value (p. 265). Thus as authentic subjectivity sublates objectivity, praxis, through which one becomes a subject, sublates theory, whereby one knows objectivity.

Cf. also Gadamer, "The art of understanding, whatever its ways and means may be, is not dependent on an explicit awareness of the rules that guide and govern it. It builds, as does rhetoric, on a natural power that everyone possesses to some degree. It is a skill in which one gifted person may surpass all others, and theory can at best only tell us why. In both rhetoric and hermeneutics, then, theory is subsequent to that out of which it is abstracted; that is to praxis." *Philosophical Hermeneutics* (Berkeley, 1976) 21.

[3]This development has been extensively traced by N. Lobkowicz in *Theory and Practice: History of a Concept from Aristotle to Marx* (South Bend, 1967) and more succinctly in *Marxism, Communism and Western Society* (New York, 1973) 8:160f. We follow Lobkowicz on this point.

[4]M. Heidegger, *Being and Time* (New York, 1962) 91–95, esp 93; also Gadamer, *Truth and Method,* 338; also B. Lonergan, *Insight,* 731–732.

[5]M. Lamb, *Solidarity with Victims* (New York, 1982) 65.

[6]*Solidarity with Victims,* 72. Cf. esp. M. Xhaufflaire, *Feuerbach et la théologie de la sécularisation* (Paris, 1970). For a survey of these positions, cf. C. Davis, "Theology and Praxis," CC 23 (1973) 154–168.

An undifferentiated submission to a nontheologically articulated notion of praxis cannot in principle produce a body of knowledge that can properly be called theology. Xhaufflaire seeks "la figure d'un Christianisme qui accepterait de nouveau de mourir a lui-même et de refuser toute continuité avec son passé tant ecclesial que libre au niveau d'un système théorique de l'identité," *Feuerbach et la théologie de la sécularisation* (p. 380). For van Oudenrijn even Metz is "theologizing when he should offer a concrete analysis," Davis (p. 165). The only manner, in fact, in which Christian theology can achieve a fusion of horizons with a given concept of praxis—assuming this to be desirable—is both from the horizon of that praxis and from the horizon of its own theoretical self-identity. Even if it wished, it cannot leap over its past. A nondialectical submission of theory to practice is impossible.

[7]G. Lukacs' theory of the party, essentially the "orthodox" one—cf. *History and Class Consciousness* (Cambridge, Mass., 1971)—subordinates the enlightenment of the workers to the demands of party organization and priorities; cf. J. Habermas, *Theory and Practice,* 25f., for a critique of Lukacs' position.

⁸Von Balthasar would see either theory- or praxis-based theologies as respectively cosmological or anthropological reductions. It is interesting to note that he seems to attach an absolute normativity to his own theological aesthetics: "This theological approach, far from being a dispensable theological by-road, is in fact the one possible approach to the heart of theology, the cosmic world-historical approach and the path of anthropological verification, being secondary aspects, complementary to it." *Love Alone* (London, 1960) 8–9.

Von Balthasar is unsympathetic both to liberation theology and its anticapitalist line; for him a social situation as such cannot be sinful and a system as complex as capitalism cannot be condemned as sinful. Cf. "Heilsgeschichtliche Ueberlegungen zur Befreiungstheologie," *Theologie der Befreiung,* ed. K. Lehmann (Einsiedeln, 1977) 198–202, 209.

By contrast, Barth was a lifelong socialist. Cf. R. Coste, *Marxist Analysis and Christian Faith* (New York, 1984) 10–13.

⁹We may repeat what we said about enlightenment consciousness being fatally flawed, as demonstrated by the "masters of suspicion." This was disclosed by uncovering its—often unconscious—practical roots. On the end of "Intellectual innocence," cf. Lonergan, *A Third Collection,* 157.

¹⁰For Lonergan, attention to the transcendental imperatives is a therapeutic process. From this point one can rejoin the Habermasian discussion on the therapeutic nature of dialogue and go on from there to a discussion of the conditions for methodological self-enlightenment in theology. This we shall attempt in chs. 9 and 10.

¹¹W. Jeanrond, "A Critical Theology of Christian Praxis," ITQ 52:2 (1985) 136, 139.

¹²Cf. *Teologia e Prática,* 368f.

¹³Theological theory could not produce this question unless it had previous methodological coherence.

¹⁴For an example of the employment of "permission," M. de Certeau, "La rupture instauratrice" *Esprit* 404 (1971) 1199–1201. Cf. also H. Carrier, "Pour une politique de la recherche dans l'Eglise" Greg 53:1 (1972) 12.

¹⁵The alternative is to imagine an autonomous ego in the manner of Fichte. K. Mannheim makes the point that "perspective" *(Situationsgebundenheit)* is more than a merely formal determination of one's thinking. It refers to qualitative elements in the structure of thought, elements which must necessarily be overlooked by a purely formal logic. "It signifies the manner in which one views an object, what one perceives in it and how one construes it in one's thinking." *Ideology and Utopia* (New York, 1936) 272.

8

The Scriptural and Christological Basis of the Privileged Perspective of the Poor

A Relative Normative Status

Hermeneutical conversation has been—at least implicitly a constantly recurring theme in the present work. As soon as any renewed theology abandons the pretense of being an "entirely new" theology, there immediately arises the question of hermeneutical interaction between the existing tradition and the new perspective. Approaching the question from the standpoint of local or contextualized theologies yields the same result: the question of relative normative status can—theologically speaking—only be resolved in a hermeneutical conversation. With the possible exception of Sobrino, the theologians expounded in this work would not seem to argue for an exclusivity in relation to their method but for a priority or relative normativity. Once again we are brought back to the conversational model, where we must face again the view proposed by Tracy, who, by transposing into theology the Gadamerian view of hermeneutics, argues that in principle there cannot be a privileged perspective. We, by contrast, tend toward the Habermasian view, which highlights the therapeutic function of critical theory in a dialogue of interpretative frameworks. Our examination of this question will take the form of outlining the philosophical paradigm provided by this famous debate on hermeneutics and then discussing its implications for theological method.

This rather long and even complicated procedure is, however, essentially a refinement, for at a more basic level there is the prima facie argument for the hermeneutical privilege of the poor found throughout biblical tradition. The point here is simple and fundamental. The Judeo-Christian concept of God was first grasped from the perspective of oppression and was constantly, even though not exclusively, refined by a critique of oppression from the point of view of the poor. This process of critical refinement is the main internal corrective of the Old Testament. The incarnation of Jesus was historically revealed by a life-praxis that favored the oppressed and crushed, just as his resurrection is constitutively the eschatological vindication of the sufferings of the unremembered and the forsaken. It is precisely the Crucified One who has been raised, and in that resurrection neither his oppression nor forsakenness are nullified, but rather, their eschatological and even divine significance are revealed.

Thus, however inadequately in the space we may allow ourselves, it will be necessary to remind ourselves of this prima facie case for the hermeneutical priority of the poor in the tradition itself. Certainly, this has been frequently alluded to in the course of the present work—even by theologians who would not accept the hermeneutical consequences. But these references were from a less hermeneutically focused standpoint. Here we enter consciously into the mutually clarifying interpenetration of perspective and thematic. Just as the biblical revelation on the privilege of the poor invites a consideration of this privilege as a hermeneutical standpoint, so the adoption of this standpoint—its rigor, validity, and necessity having been established—makes possible a new reading of the very heart of the tradition. We "arrive where we started and know the place for the first time." In this manner there is a mutual process of refinement, codetermination, and verification.

The Old Testament God of the Poor and Oppressed

The historical roots of the Judeo-Christian religious attitude to poverty, property, and equality are probably to be found in the nomadic past of the people of God, where kinship and not ownership was the key value. What is of particular significance is the fact that the transition from a nomadic to a settled way of life with consequent property rights did not—at least at the level of aspiration—undo this but, rather, intensified it. There can scarcely be any doubt that the deciding factor in this extraordinary fidelity to the concept of brotherly equality, to the exclusion of poverty, is rooted in the Exodus experience:[1] the realization that Yahweh had manifested his election and promise to his people in and through and because of their oppression. The way to appropriate the revelation of the God who favored his people in their—figurative—"strangerhood, widowhood, and orphanhood" was to favor the stranger, the widow, and the orphan. It resulted in the values of a communitarian, just, and merciful way of life being enshrined in the covenant with Yahweh.

Undoubtedly, the change to landed property was an enormous innovation for the people of God. But there are several remarkable features, together pointing to a fundamentally egalitarian and communitarian ethos. Parity and equality mark the division of land; it is owned not by individuals but by the clan. This is an ethical principle to the extent of forbidding sale in perpetuity.[2] Thus, in terms of socioethical aspiration, we are dealing with a society that constitutively expresses its covenant with God by holding to the principles of parity and equality to the exclusion of class and property-based privilege.

N. Gottwald has highlighted how Yahwistic faith has a socioeconomic rather than a mythical referent, indicative of a notion of God accessible only within the construction of a just and fraternal way of life:

> "Yahweh" is the historically concretized, primordial power to establish and sustain social equality in the face of counteroppression from without and against provincial and nonegalitarian tendencies from within the society. "The chosen People" is the distinctive self-consciousness of a society of equals created in the intertribal order and demarcated from a primarily centralized and stratified surrounding world. "Covenant" is the bonding of decentralized social groups in a larger society of equals committed to cooperation without authoritarian leadership and a way of symbolizing the locus of sovereignty in such a society of equals. "Eschatology," or hope for the future, is the sustained commitment of fellow tribesmen to a society of equals with the confidence and determination that this way of life can prevail against great environmental odds.[3]

Clearly this aspiration failed, or rather, deteriorated, as a consequence of greed, especially during the rise of the monarchy. The result is a new social order with new economic conditions no longer mediating the covenant with God. The divided society that resulted, with its implicit acceptance of destitution and marginalization, contradicted the covenant with God and created a religious climate that, relative to the God of the covenant, was a practical idolatry.

The Deuteronomic reform is essentially a return to the will of God through fidelity to the covenant, which is constitutively a corrective response to the inequalities and injustices that had crept in. Its ideal and aim are remarkably clear: "There shall be no poor among you!" The same demand for a just, fraternal, egalitarian way of life is enshrined in the code of the covenant (Exod 20:22–23:33) as well as in the code of Holiness (Lev 17–26). Here is repeated the clear intention of land parity, the restoration of alienated property, and the liberation of slaves as the real meaning of Jubilee—regrettably, seldom if ever observed.

This nonobservance of the covenant with Yahweh—never merely a ritual celebration but coextensively a socioeconomic program—forms the background to the prophetic outcries and denunciations of the oppression of the poor that follows on injustice, fraud, and the monopolizing of capital and land. Greed breaks the bond of fraternity and destroys the covenant with God, for which God will call the powerful to judgment. Text upon text may be quoted to indicate how the prophets rallied to the side of the poor and denounced extravagance, injustice, inequality, and greed. Fidelity to the covenant was fidelity to the communitarian, fraternal understanding of society. Just as God had favored the Hebrews in their oppression, the prophets who spoke for God critically corrected his domestication in idolatry by expressing his salvific nature from the side of the poor. His salvific will is crowded out by the acquisition of power. It can reveal itself only to the poor and to those who love them.

Background to the Ministry of Jesus

Although a historiographical study of the context of the life and ministry of Jesus is a secondary source for Christian life and faith, without it what we know of his history can easily be reduced to ethical-religious teaching.

First-century Palestine[4] was a country of deep social divisions, foreign domination, excessive taxation, and the maldistribution of land, as well as an ideologically and religiously reinforced caste system. The population included a vast rural "proletariat" as well as a significant body of urban destitutes living in a country of considerable resources but demoralized by the extravagant opulence of the few and by a corrupted priesthood.

This had come to a head as a result of the cruelty, extravagance, and institutionalized violence of the reign of Herod the Great. The centralization of land holdings, begun after the era of the Judges, had reached alarming proportions under his reign. This background of wealthy landowners and impoverished peasants constantly faced with the prospect of joining the ever-increasing band of day laborers is assumed in so much of the teaching of Jesus, especially in the Gospel of Luke, that it must have been the dominant sociopolitical backdrop to his preaching.

Jerusalem was the urban focus to which rich and poor came on pilgrimage out of religious devotion. Here the spectacle of a glittering and decadent court contrasted with a sizable urban proletariat subsisting largely on the religious significance of the city. The priesthood was an equally decadent institution, noted for venality. There are numerous records of the high-priestly office being bought and sold. The very loyalty to the Temple, strongest among the common people, was yet another way of exploitation, the poor being the victims of merchants, money changers, and clergy alike. The action of Jesus in cleansing the Temple, and therefore, the repercussion of this action in terms of his death, cannot be understood without reference to this situation.

Taxation is a constantly recurring gospel theme, which to the people represented an insupportable financial burden as well as a religious affront. While the religious tax was acceptable in principle, the secular tax was a double impoverishment—it paid for the wars, whose social consequences, including expropriation of land, led to greater social divisions. The right to farm tax was a feature of life. The Gospels frequently refer to the hatred of the people for such tax collectors—not primarily because they were foreigners but because of their greed and dishonesty.

More fundamentally, perhaps, the community of Judaism at the time of Jesus was dominated by the concept of the maintenance of racial purity. The division of the people along social lines was ruled by this principle, which mirrored very closely, though not exactly, the economic differentiation. People, especially priests, were obsessed with their racial purity. This led to a climate where a whole series of situations and experiences carried social stigma in public opinion—precisely the ones entered into provocatively and prophetically by Jesus. A whole gamut of trades was despised, and their practitioners were exposed to social depredation. This stigma effectively excluded people from any public position of responsibility or respect. The hatred for the Samaritans—a group frequently privileged by Jesus in his parables and actions—derives primarily from their racial origins rather than from doctrinal aberrations.

This situation of grave injustice and division was, if anything, heightened and intensified by the ideological hegemony exercised by the scribes and Pharisees. The scribes may be described as a new "upper-middle class," and the balance of power and influence had moved their way during the time of Jesus. They were an elite of ordained scholars who dominated the Pharisaic party in the Sanhedrin. They effectively created, transmitted, and controlled the tradition to which the common people felt conscience bound. This hegemony was intensified by the prevailing legalism of the Pharisee party, whose influential leaders were all scribes. Because of its unrivaled following, that party exercised an enormous influence over the consciousness of the people at large, which served as a legitimation mechanism for much of the oppressive power in society. In particular, the delineation they drew between themselves and the unlettered masses, who were "ignorant of the Law," amounted effectively to a distinction of caste. Righteousness and salvation were reserved to the keepers of the Law. It was specifically from the perspective of the "publicans and sinners" that Jesus articulated his inclusive concept of the reign of God, and it was precisely as a consequence of this that he was crucified.

The Ministry of Jesus

There is now virtual unanimity that the central concept in the ministry of Jesus was the reign of God: "As an evangelizer, Christ first of all proclaims a kingdom, the Kingdom of God; and this is so important that, by comparison, everything else becomes the rest, which is given in addition. Only the Kingdom therefore is absolute, and it makes everything else relative. The Lord will delight in describing in many ways the happiness of belonging to this kingdom (a paradoxical happiness which is made up of things that the world rejects)."[5]

The decisive feature of this kingdom is that it is *good news for the poor*. The admonition not to be scandalized by Jesus in his making present of this kingdom can only mean that his proclamation in word and deed, which privileged the poor, who were considered marginalized and unworthy, was in fact highly offensive to the prevailing wisdom. The very description of Jesus as the "friend of sinners" confirms this: "We can now say that Jesus' following consisted predominantly of the disreputable; the *amne ha-ares,* the uneducated, the ignorant, whose religious ignorance and moral behavior stood in the way of their access to salvation according to the conviction of the time."[6]

To understand who these people were and why Jesus favored them in his proclamation of the reign of God, we can look to the powerful significance of his celebrated table-fellowship with the officially unrighteous. This parable in action can serve as a code for the whole of his ministry and his anticipation of the definitive reign of God.[7] We must see this, first, against the background already outlined, and second, not solely as a kind of humanitarian gesture indicative of his compassion but as an expression of his mission, message, and being. These meals are prophetic gestures, which both promise and anticipate the eschatological banquet. Theologically, the consummation of God's universal salvific project is mediated through solidarity with the marginalized. Fraternity and restored communion with the oppressed is the efficacious sign and promise of God's forgiveness and the restoration of communion between God and all people. The need for this restoration is evident precisely in the exclusion from human communion of the downtrodden, the despised, and the marginalized.

It is crucial that our understanding of Jesus' preferential involvement with the oppressed does not stop short at seeing it solely or even primarily in terms of Jesus' sovereign compassion for all people but especially the poor and forgotten. It goes deeper than this, though it does include it. The poor are the privileged ones because the reign of God comes to pass in and through them and in favor of them. It is from their perspective that the reign of God—restoring communion between all people and with God himself—can best be seen. The exigencies of the coming eschatological kingdom cannot be grasped from the perspective of the wealthy, the privileged, the righteous, or the various elites precisely because the basis of their privilege lies in factors that ensure that marginalization and oppression of others which God's coming reign seeks to abolish.

J. Jeremias,[8] despite his groundbreaking historical-exegetical work on this question, seems theologically incorrect in his understanding of the privilege of the poor. He argues that it derives from the fact that (a) the poor are grateful, (b) the self-righteousness of the justified makes them further from God, and (c) the graciousness of God is infinite. The fundamental difficulty with this line of argumentation is its implicit horizon of individual salvation: the universal inclusivist aspect of eschatology has been individualized. In fact, the poor are not always grateful, for sometimes part of their poverty and oppression is an internalization of the prevailing ethos of greed. The infinite graciousness of God extends to all people: the privilege of the poor does not mean that any given poor person is loved more by God than a rich person. The issue is the manner in which the meaning of the reign of God and the actual acceptance of God's sovereign saving graciousness is accessible to all in and through those who yearn for a transformation of the present order and its replacement by an order of fraternal and egalitarian solidarity. This longing, even though not present with differentiated consciousness in the heart of every poor person considered as an individual, is only present with authentic eschatological urgency among those who are poor and wait for God to inaugurate his reign of gracious love in favor of their aspiration for a new quality of human solidarity, and among those who in different ways have espoused the cause of the poor and, in doing so, have become poor in spirit.

Certainly, the same hope for a fraternal world expressing the care of God for all people is also present in the hearts of many who by reason of education, personal gifts, or life situation are not poor. But this hope cannot free itself from delusion, paternalism, and a merely conceptual commitment to the historical realization of sisterhood/brotherhood under the fatherhood of God unless it is rooted in a real and true dialogue of *koinōnia* with those who are actually poor and suffering. In short, it demands a preferential option for the poor such as we have outlined in the fifth chapter of the present work.

"Blessed Are the Poor"

This seminal statement of Jesus, which sums up the gospel passage that in turn sums up his teaching, has proven notoriously difficult in the history of exegesis.

We may proceed with J. Dupont[9] by noting that the divergence between Matthew and Luke derives from an earlier redaction, which each evangelist has elaborated in a different way. The interpretation that the Matthean redaction is in the direction of spelling out the ethical-spiritual implications of the Beatitudes is supported by the fact that the Beatitudes proper to Matthew possess an ethical aspect. Rather than announcing the blessedness of the deprived in the present moment, they promise it to the virtuous in the world to come. In like manner, the placing of the maledictions proper to the third Gospel suppose Luke's particular interpretation. The messianic kingdom favors the poor. It is not good news to the powerful.

The term "poor" speaks of a class in both social and religious terms. The poor, in this sense, are distinguished both by their social oppression and by their total dependence upon the will of God. The inseparability of these aspects means that the notion of poverty can neither be spiritualized nor expanded to include the *"bons riches."*[10] Any semantic evolution of the term "poor" to include a religious meaning is a superimposition rather than a substitution. The valid spiritualizing dimension can never become an abstraction from material conditions.

The promise of the kingdom to the poor is not mere compensation, for Jesus is announcing a messianic blessedness that has already begun. Rather than pointing primarily to the next world, the roots of the Beatitudes in the Isaian messianic hope point to the present moment. Jesus fulfills the messianic hope, and the specific task of the Messiah is defined in relation to the disinherited of this world. This point is borne out by the quasi-total incompatibility between the exigencies of the kingdom and the attachment to riches found throughout the Gospels. It is the counterpoint of the privilege of the poor. God, as is evident from the Magnificat, reverses and inverts the human condition.

The meaning of the term "poor" in the Beatitudes cannot therefore be made to coincide with "just" or "pious": the use of the word is in the real and concrete sense of the term.[11] Dupont rejects the view that the poor addressed by the Beatitudes are saved because they have fulfilled moral conditions. Equally, he rejects the view that the poor are privileged because of some interior disposition. Such approaches warp the meaning of the Beatitudes. For Dupont, the basis of the privilege of the poor is not found in any conceptual idealization of their poverty but in God himself and specifically in the manner in which he exercises his royal function for the sake of the weak. Their real privilege lies not in their justice but in God's. This is paralleled by the privilege of the sinners precisely because Jesus is sent to them.

Certainly, this original meaning is modified in a new situation. The emphasis shifts from the manner in which God acts "for the sake of his holy name" to the dispositions of those who would enter his kingdom. Then the privilege of the poor is seen not in their oppression, which appeals to the justice of God, but in their spirituality, which awaits an eschatological reward. This is an extremely early development. But in relation to the original meaning of the Beatitudes, it represents a considerable shift.

This development continues with the individualization of eschatological perspective. The emphasis is now on the religious disposition of poor Christians, whose just behavior corresponds to the divine will. "Poor" now comes to mean humble and docile before God, just as Jesus himself is "meek and humble of heart." This spiritualizing redactional process must not obscure the fundamental thrust of the Beatitudes, which can be retrieved today because of the globalization of poverty and the ecclesiological developments that point to a Church existing less for itself than for the kingdom of God.

> Thus this good news announced to the poor takes its true meaning in function of a "theological" presupposition. It is a matter of a certain conception of God and His reign. God is indeed the creator of all men: rich, poor, strong, weak, oppressors and oppressed; they are all His sons. But God is not neutral. Fully in accord with His compassionate mercy, His "Royal" "Justice" is partisan in favor of the small, the humble, the weak,

the crushed. In His kingdom the poor cannot be other than privileged and that by reason of the manner whereby He intends to exercise His royal power.[12]

The "poor" of the Beatitudes therefore has a meaning with inseparable material and spiritual dimensions, even though not equivalently. In the former dimension, the term refers concretely to those who want, who are disadvantaged, who are powerless, overburdened, and oppressed. In the latter dimension, it refers to those who wait on God, who depend on him, those who having lost faith in human institutions—both religious and secular—depend on God alone to vindicate them. Consequently, the specific meaning of the term "poor" in the Beatitudes is those actually poor and oppressed people who, having only God to depend on, do so with a messianic hope. In short, the poor of the Gospels are the materially poor who are also poor in spirit. They are not just the materially poor *simpliciter,* much less those comfortable people aiming at a putative spiritual poverty, but the actual oppressed, disadvantaged, and powerless who have the spiritual poverty of those who truly depend on God alone. They are the ones who grasp the reign of God and see it as vindicating the rights of the oppressed, not in granting them hegemony over their erstwhile oppressors, but in creating conditions for a truly fraternal way of life. The exaltation of the humble and the casting down of the mighty occur not in a crude reversal of the previous relationship of domination but in the emergence of solidarity. The reign of God comes in favor of all by coming in favor of the poor, in a manner understood by those poor who are also poor in spirit and of whom Mary is the exemplar.

The Privilege of the Poor in the New Testament Tradition

Much recent research[13] indicates that the standard picture of early Christianity as poor, egalitarian, and marginalized, entering the upper strata of the Roman Empire only after the Constantinian Peace, is probably more romantic than true. The New Testament texts themselves are not the product of an unsophisticated and unlettered people.

The pattern is quite clear in the case of the Pauline communities. Paul's postsynagogue preaching is clearly an attempt to bring faith in Jesus to a sophisticated urban culture. What is intriguing in this context is the contrast between Paul and his communities. Clearly a socially privileged person, Paul voluntarily chooses simplicity for the sake of authenticity—both on religious grounds and as a means of identifying himself in the educated pagan mind as the equivalent of a dignified philosopher. The communities seemed less pleased by this stance. This attitude was probably governed by many factors, but the predominant Hellenistic attitude to manual labor was certainly one of them.

In similar vein, the oft-quoted charge of Celsus that Christians limited their appeal to the poor was first questioned by Deismann, who argued that the New Testament textual style indicated authors and audience from the middle classes. This view was qualified by Judge, who argued for a social mix. Subsequently, this view has, in turn, been modified by Theisen, who argues for a majority from the lower classes and a minority from the upper classes. On this basis, Theisen characterizes the Pauline Corinthian community as socially stratified, similar to the surrounding culture. By analyzing the theological issues in the Corinthian Church, for example, eating of sacrificed meat and the split in the agapeistic celebrations, he has confirmed how theological debate can never be divorced from social reality.

Building on this research, W. Meeks, who gives less importance than Theisen to linking social and theological issues, paints a similar picture, though with a focus on that segment of society that was upwardly mobile, and he singles this out as the group most active in Pauline circles. Quite clearly, however, the fact of a social mix is already obvious from the internal evidence of the New Testament's text,[14] but what is equally clear is a shift from the original Jesus movement, with its roots in the dispossessed peasantry of first-century Palestine. As the deutero-Pauline and Johannine literature indicate, the trend in early Catholicism was in the direction of stabilizing and organizing with a relative loss of apocalyptic urgency, reflecting the delay in the parousia and reflected, in turn, in a diminished emphasis on the privileged role of the poor.

Yet what is equally extraordinary and central to the issue under discussion is the manner in which the New Testament tradition, written out of the *Sitz im Leben* of the early Church, continued to emphasize the privilege of the poor in the plan of salvation.[15]

Despite its relative spiritualization of the Beatitudes as well as its vindication of Jesus as the new Moses, Matthew's Gospel is still the text that identifies the Son of Man with the least of his brethren. The privilege of the poor is a totally dominant theme in the Lucan tradition: theirs is the kingdom, and those who do not become like them through a radical renunciation of privilege cannot enter it. The aspiration for a fraternal communality of life and goods remains a dominant theme of his interpretation of the early community.

Paul is not generally recognized as an exponent of the privilege of the poor, but this oversight is due primarily to the reduction of his staurocentric Christology to a merely noetic mystery. We have only to reflect on the concrete significance of the "scandal" of the cross in Pauline soteriology to see the sociopolitical implications of his view of salvation consistent with this. The "cross" functions in Paul's thought as the "kingdom" does in the preaching of Jesus. It radically undermines any pretension to ethical or social superiority based either on culture or religion. Thus, it is a symbol of radical egalitarianism before God, mediated by the powerless and demanding an all-encompassing fraternal love as its concrete expression. Paul seems more sociopolitically conservative than Luke, but in demanding a radical fraternity in the agape, he communicates his real social vision. In the Eucharistic meal a transformation of societal relationships takes place, and this sacramental integration is intended to have sociohistorical repercussions.[16] Paul keeps us in no doubt that a putative Eucharistic community seeking to celebrate the Lord's resurrection without reference to the poor is an abomination.

In James the privilege of the poor is more blunt and forthright; the poor are the chosen ones. Their privilege is vindicated with a vigor reminiscent of the prophets and matched only by the open and vehement rejection of pseudoreligion that sits easily with an attachment to riches. The rich are openly described as oppressors: the maledictions of the Lucan tradition become forthright denunciation. Undefiled religion involves an option for the poor.

The Christological Basis of the Privilege of the Poor

At the heart of all Christology stands the cross: It is not the whole of Christology but the point of verification of all Christology and, by extension, of all explicitly Christian "Theo-logy."[17] God is the God of the cross, the significance of which is revealed in the resurrection. Without thereby reducing the resurrection to the continuation of the "cause of Jesus," it is crucial to see the cross first in historical terms, that is, in function of Jesus' options and praxis. Otherwise, the result will be a solely noetic Christology that will remember only the vocabulary of Jesus but not his praxis. The consequence is the Christ of domesticated religion, who, had he ever existed, would never have been crucified in the first place.

The ministry of Jesus, exemplified in his table-fellowship with the excluded, was a scandal of such total proportions, which so threatened to undermine the Law, that is, the accepted religious ideology, that either Jesus or the Law would have to be destroyed. This is why, on the cross, God has abolished the Law and replaced it with grace, not by some suprahistorical divine voluntarism, but rather by revealing in the poverty of the crucified Jesus the consequences of the Law. The Law canonized privilege and marginalization, not directly at the material level but at the ideological level, which legitimated marginalization at every level and stood as a pseudotheological statement that access to God was on the basis of privilege—the privilege of knowing and keeping the Law. What is implicit in the praxis of Jesus is that access to the God of sovereign universal compassion, who is the true God, is possible only on the basis of a conversion to solidarity with those who are marginalized by all other concepts of God, even when these are couched in a facile universalism. The path to universality is by way of solidarity with the excluded: only a solidarity that privileges them can embrace all.

To believe in the lordship of Jesus Christ—which is to claim that in his life, death, and resurrection God is revealed in a unique, irreplaceable, and unsurpassable way—is to believe that the praxis of Jesus reveals God in an equivalently unique way. For Jesus was crucified because of the way he lived and the options he took. God's eternal salvific will unfolds in and through the wonder of human freedom. God's "deliverance" of his Son occurred in his Son's acceptance, as intrinsic to his incarnation, of being the victim of the mindlessness of the powerful. To believe in the resurrection, the eschatological significance of the cross, is to believe in the eschatological significance of the option of Jesus for the poor.

Consequently, the option for the poor is the concretization of the option for the crucified Jesus: Our faith in the cross of Christ is inseparably solidarity with the oppressed. That God is revealed in the cross of Christ means that the poor, "in whom Christ is crucified until the end of time," are the *locus theologicus* par excellence. Christ identified himself with them. He articulated the reign of God from the perspective of their yearnings and became himself the poor person par excellence. Since this perspective is crucial and privileged in facilitating the realization of what God and his kingdom are, it is necessarily a privileged hermeneutical standpoint of Christian theology.

Concluding Remarks

Our necessarily schematic overview of the privilege of the poor in revelation illustrates how the specifically Christian concept of God is rooted in the experience of the liberation of the poor, and when threatened by domestication or practical idolatry, it is retrieved by rediscovering it from that perspective. Were it not for the contemporary debate in hermeneutics, our case could rest here. Since, however, the concept of dialogue in hermeneutical conversation has been summoned to exclude in principle any a priori claim to hermeneutical privilege, it is to this question, as exemplified by the Gadamer-Habermas debate, that we must now turn our attention.

Notes

[1] J. Severino-Croatto, *Exodus: A Hermeneutics of Freedom* (New York, 1981); also "L'importance socio-historique et hermeneutique de l'Exode," Con 209:7–8 (1987) 151–159.

[2] "Land must not be sold in perpetuity, for the land belongs to me and you are only strangers and guests. You will allow a right of redemption on all your landed property" (Lev 25:23). Catholic social teaching since Leo XIII has gradually recovered this fundamentally communitarian approach to the ownership of property. With John Paul II's *Laborem exercens*, "the right to private property is inconceivable without responsibilities to the common good. It is subordinated to the higher principle which states that goods are meant for all." AAS 73 (1981) 625f., n. 19, we may be said to have recovered the biblical thrust. Cf. also ch. 5 above.

[3] N. Gottwald, *The Tribes of Yahweh: A Sociology of the Religion of Liberated Israel, 1250–1050 B.C.* (New York, 1979) 692.

⁴Here we are following principally S. Freyne, *Galilee: From Alexander the Great to Hadrian* (Notre Dame, 1980) as well as J. Jeremias, *Jerusalem zur Zeit Jesus* (Goettingen, 1962); English trans., *Jerusalem in the Time of Jesus* (London, 1969). *See also* H. Daniel-Rops, *Jesus dans son Temps* (Paris, 1950); A. Nolan, *Jesus Before Christianity* (London, 1979); and J. Cassidy, *Jesus, Politics and Society* (New York, 1979).

⁵Paul VI, *Evangelii nuntiandi,* AAS 68 (1975) 5–76, n. 8.

⁶J. Jeremias, *New Testament Theology* (London, 1969) 1:112.

⁷N. Perrin, *Rediscovering the Teaching of Jesus* (London, 1967) 102–108. Perrin is cited on this point because of his "minimalist" methodology in looking for the kernel of the NT Jesus tradition. While not fully agreeing with his method, for many pericopes not meeting his rigorous conditions could be original, it does have the merit of reconstructing what is historically certain.

⁸*New Testament Theology* 1:119–120.

⁹*Les Béatitudes,* vol. 1 (Louvain, 1954), vols. 2 and 3 (Paris, 1969). The second and third volumes are an expansion of the original work: 'L'orientation initiale s'est peut-être précisée au cours du temps; nous n'avons pas l'impression qu'elle ait changé" (3:7). Cf. 1:90, 90, n. 2, 78, 110.

¹⁰Ibid., 142–147.

¹¹*Les Béatitudes,* 1:291, "Ceux que les béatitudes disent 'pauvres' le sont au sens réel et concret du mot." As to reducing the sense of poor to interior dispositions, cf. vol. 2, pp. 141–142, "Nous pensons que cette optique gauchit le sens des béatitudes." With regard to the spiritualizing development, cf. vol. 3, p. 28, "Le glissement est considérable par rapport a la signification originelle des béatitudes."

¹²*Les Béatitudes,* 3:669 (trans. ours).

¹³*See* R. Grant, *Early Christianity and Society* (New York, 1972); E. A. Judge, *The Social Pattern of Christian Groups in the First Century* (Tyndale, 1968); W. Meeks, *The First Urban Christians: The Social World of the Apostle Paul* (New Haven & London, 1983); C. Osiek, *What Are They Saying About the Social Setting of the New Testament* (New York, 1984); R. H. Smith, "Were the Early Christians Middle-Class: A Sociological Analysis of the New Testament," in N. K. Gottwald, ed., *The Bible and Liberation* (New York, 1983) 441–446; and G. Theisen, *The Social Setting of Pauline Christianity* (Philadelphia, 1982).

¹⁴*See* esp. Rom 15:25–27; Acts 4:32–37; I Cor 11:20; II Cor 8:13–14; Jas 2:1–9; I Pet 3:13.

¹⁵J. C. Gager concludes his "Social Description and Sociological Explanation in the Study of Early Christianity" by citing Judge: "Modern Christians, uneasy about the respectability of a faith that is supposed to have revolutionary implications, like to cultivate the idea that it first flourished among the depressed sections of society" (p. 51), and he adds, "Conversely, modern interpreters who advocate a social upgrading of the early Christians should be on guard lest their own respectability find its way into the machinery of their social analysis." *The Bible and Liberation,* 440.

¹⁶*The Social Setting of Pauline Christianity,* 164–167.

¹⁷On this question *see* esp. M. Kaehler, *The So-called Historical Jesus and the Historic Biblical Christ* (Philadelphia, 1964). For a political interpretation of the Lutheran theology of the cross, cf. J. Moltmann, *The Crucified God* (London, 1974) esp. pp. 325f. On the centrality of the cross in Christian life and theology, cf. G. O'Collins, *The Calvary Christ* (London, 1977). The principal merit of Moltmann's work was to reexamine the applicability of the "god" of philosophical theism to Christian faith (cf. 214f).

9

Dialogue and Hermeneutical Privilege

In a world composed of fair-minded people bereft of vested interests, which are linked in different ways to systems of oppression and marginalization, a theological conversation could be expected to be simply an ongoing process of mutual clarification and enrichment. But such a world does not exist, and an age of intellectual innocence that cheerfully produced theories without reference to the social and psychological roots of its discourse is long gone. In however limited a way, each of us knows that she or he has internalized structures of marginalization, whether as oppressor or oppressed. We know, too, how insight dawns on us that our own discourse, whether theological or otherwise, is distorted through being unconsciously—in the very structure of its grammar, one might say—either a justification of our privilege or a reinforcement of our oppression. If such an insight has dawned on us, then we have experienced how the process in question is quite different from the simple acquisition of more information, or even from the mutual clarification and enrichment of views that occur in the conversation between partners of roughly equivalent perspectives. We experience, in short, that it is a therapeutic experience—whether structured or not—that involves a moment of vulnerability or liminality, during which we gain a precious insight into the psychosocial roots of our discourse and consequently into its distortedness. Reflection on this experience shows that we were not led to the new level of insight simply by rhetoric.

In a not dissimilar way, the claim that a theology elaborated from the perspective of the poor has a hermeneutical privilege over theologies with a different sociopolitical rootedness—or for that matter, over a theology unconscious of having any such rootedness at all—implies the view that theological conversation can be—and is—distorted through its own partial rootedness in structures of oppression. As a result, we are led back to the limitations of the conversational model of theological hermeneutics and therefore to the limitations of the Gadamerian theory of hermeneutics as critiqued by Habermas. A résumé of the debate between these two offers a sort of philosophical paradigm to the present discussion on theological method as to whether all conversation partners are strictly equal or whether some, because of the rootedness of their discourse in the struggle of the poor, possess a certain kind of hermeneutical privilege.

Toward a Hermeneutical Theory

In outlining Gadamer's theory of hermeneutics, we may conveniently begin with his rejection of the Schleiermacher-Dilthy identification of the meaning of a text with the subjective intention of the author.[1] Their mistake is the Enlightenment's assumption of the autonomous ego, which can extricate itself from its own historicity and the prejudices that are part of it. For Gadamer, one's historicity is an ontological rather than an accidental factor in interpretation and is thus constitutive of the process of understanding. The historicity of our existence entails that prejudices, in the literal sense of the word, constitute the initial directedness of our whole ability to experience.

In Gadamer's view, the prejudice to be overcome is the Enlightenment's prejudice against prejudice. The temporal distance between text and interpreter is not a negative factor to be overcome but a productive ground of understanding. It is the inverse of the putative neutralized prejudice—free consciousness that would guarantee the objectivity of scientific knowledge. This ideal of knowledge—supreme from Descartes until Heidegger—is itself a prejudice. Thus for Gadamer, understanding is not reconstruction but mediation. Understanding is to be thought of not so much as an action of one's subjectivity but as the placing of oneself within a process of tradition in which past and present are constantly fused. The past is not simply to be overcome but instead provides the effective history *(Wirkungsgeschichte)* that makes possible the conversation between text and interpreter.

In this manner, he seeks to abolish any "abstract opposition" between knowledge and tradition and to vindicate the latter in a critical manner, insisting that only a naive and unreflective historicism in hermeneutics would seek to abolish tradition. "At the beginning of all historical hermeneutics, then, the abstract antithesis between tradition and historical research, between history and knowledge must be discarded. The effect of a living tradition and the effect of historical study must constitute a unity, the analysis of which would reveal only a texture of reciprocal relationships. . . . In other words, we hope to inquire into the element of tradition in the historical relation and inquire into its hermeneutical productivity."[2]

Horizons are the presupposition of finite understanding, and understanding is always a process of *Horizontsversmeltzung*—the "fusion of these horizons which we imagine to exist by themselves."[3] The past ceases to appear as a fixed object of study and is revealed as a source of possible meanings.

Gadamer places great stress on the analogy of the game in explaining hermeneutical understanding. The to-and-fro movement in which the players are absorbed, as a paradigm of true dialogue, is, he argues, a truer reflection of understanding—since both text and interpreter are involved—than is the model of methodologically controlled investigation. Thus, the search is not for what is presumed to be "behind" the text but for what the text itself says. There is active reciprocity and equality of involvement. Concentration on the partner rather than on the subject subverts the dialogical character of interpretation. Prejudices disappear by concentrating on the truth in the otherness of the text.

In this process, the priority lies not with the *mens auctoris* but with the question the text sought to answer and the provocation of the interpreter to question further in that direction. Thus, the horizon of the text is transcended, and in fusing it with the interpreter's, his horizon is similarly transcended. In Platonic terms—and the Socratic dialogues remain, for Gadamer, the examples *par excellence* of the process he seeks to describe—text and interpreter are both led by the Logos: "This is not an external matter of simply adjusting our tools nor is it even right to say that the partners adapt themselves to one another but, rather, in the successful conversation they both come under the influence of the truth of the object and are thus bound to one another in a new community . . . a transformation into a communion, in which we do not remain what we were."[4]

The *mens auctoris* approach to hermeneutics subjectifies meaning and understanding and renders tradition unintelligible. The meaning of a text does not depend solely on the contingencies of the author, "for it is always partly determined also by the historical situation of the interpreter and hence by the totality of the objective course of history . . . hence the interpreter can and must, often understand more than he (the author). But this is of fundamental importance. Not occasionally only, but always, the meaning of a text goes beyond its author. That is why understanding is not merely a reproductive but always a productive attitude as well."[5]

The work lives in its presentations, which are not extrinsic but disclosive. There is no definitive interpretation. Not only does a text or tradition not exclude interpretation; it requires it in order to convey meaning—and it must be interpreted differently precisely so that in changed circumstances, it can say the same thing.

Understanding is thus seen to be episodic, transsubjective, and linguistic. For Gadamer, being that can be understood is language. Language and the understanding of transmitted meaning are one and the same process. We do not first have extralinguistic understanding, which we subsequently express in language. Language is not a cipher but is inseparable from understanding as a structure of being-in-the-world. Linguisticality as an ontological condition of understanding further presupposes immersion in tradition.

The linguisticality of understanding transcends the limits of any particular language. It is the concrete use of language in conversation that promotes the horizon of understanding, which thus emerges as transsubjective and dialogical. As dialogue, language is not the possession of the participant but the medium of understanding. Insight is possible in conversation because words, due to their relationality to the whole of being, have around them a "circle of the unexpressed," drawing the partners into the "infinity of the unsaid."

Gadamer explicitly acknowledges his proximity to the later Wittgenstein who had abandoned the *Tractatus,* replacing the ideal of a universal grammar in terms of a logical calculus with the concept of language games where the meaning of words emerge in their usage. For both, language games exist only in interpersonal communication. Gadamer develops this, however, in describing the dynamic character of language, which communication discloses and interprets without ever exhausting. What is understood can affect the form or rules that compose one's horizons.

Hermeneutics and Critical Theory

In outlining Habermas' position with regard to Gadamer's hermeneutics, we must first stress their common ground. They are united in overcoming the supplanting of *praxis* by *techné* and the instrumentalization of reason in scientism; in upholding the rootedness of reason in historicity; and in promoting conditions for genuine distortion-free communication.[6] In essence, Habermas agrees with Gadamer on the intertranslatability of different language structures over against the view of linguisticality as an individual totality. Consequently, he is in agreement with Gadamer that translation between languages, rather than socialization into a primary language, is the paradigm of hermeneutic understanding: "The understanding of a language is not yet of itself a real understanding *(Verstehen)* and does not include an interpretative process but is an accomplishment of life *(Lebensvollzug)*. For you understand a language by living in it. . . . Thus the hermeneutical problem is not one of the correct mastery of a language but of the proper understanding of what takes place through the medium of language."[7]

This agreement continues in Habermas' insistence on historicality: language exists only as transmitted *(tradierte)*. For tradition reflects on a large scale the lifelong socialization of individuals in their language. Their common ground on the historicality of understanding and the vindication of tradition's *Wirkungsgeschichte* allows a critique—in Habermas' work—of a sociology allegedly free of history and seeking to articulate a technical mastery over the future.

When we come to the issue of praxis, the debate becomes interesting. Gadamer had insisted on "application" being constitutive of interpretative understanding, the applicative moment being universal and necessary. Thus, both he and Habermas are united in the view that interpretation "is linked with transcendental necessity to the articulation of an action-orienting self-understanding." Habermas would, however, distance himself from the position that argues that submission to tradition is a condition of finite consciousness on the grounds that finite understanding can never extricate itself from its own history. For then hermeneutics would seem to subordinate interpretative understanding to participation in the "profound movement of human existence" as mediated by tradition. Habermas has reservations about what he sees as the conservative undertones here: "The hermeneutic insight is certainly correct viz., the insight that understanding—no matter how controlled it may be—cannot simply leap over the interpreter's relationship to tradition. But . . . it does not follow that the medium of tradition is not profoundly altered by scientific reflection. . . . This type of reflection . . . in grasping the genesis of the tradition from which it proceeds and on which it turns back . . . shakes the dogmatism of life-praxis."[8]

What Habermas fears here is a tendency towards absolutizing language and tradition so that participation and dialogue are always given precedence over distantiation and critique: "Reflection does not wrestle with the facticity of transmitted norms without leaving a trace. . . . Reflection recalls that path of authority along which grammars of language games were dogmatically inculcated as rules for interpreting the world and for action. In this process, the element of authority that was simply domination can be stripped away."

For Habermas, hermeneutic interpretation must be joined to a critique of ideology: "Language as tradition is evidently dependent on social processes that are not reducible to normative relationships. Language is also a medium of domination and social power. It serves to legitimate relations of organized force. . . . Language is also ideological. Here it is not a question of deceptions within a language but of deception with language as such. Hermeneutical experience . . . changes into the critique of ideology."[9]

If social processes are not to be sublimated into cultural traditions, hermeneutic understanding must be linked to social analysis. The linguistic infrastructure of a society is codetermined by constraints in the areas of labor and domination. These contraints are not only the object of interpretations, for they also affect the very grammar of interpretation. "Cultural tradition then loses the appearance of an absolute that a self-sufficient hermeneutics falsely lends to it. Tradition as a whole can be assigned its place . . . in its relation to the systems of social labor and political domination."[10] Not to do so would risk reducing social inquiry to understanding the sense of the terms employed *(Sinnverstehen)*, as if linguistically articulated consciousness could completely determine the material conditions of life.

Universalizing the Scope of Hermeneutics

Gadamer's reply comes framed in a discourse on the universal scope and function of hermeneutics. He begins by acknowledging that the paradigm of translation does not fully come to grips with the manifoldness of what language means in human existence, and he recognizes that the questions raised by Habermas demand reflection on the relation between hermeneutical reflection and the methods of the social sciences.

On this point, however, he accuses Habermas of seeking to make hermeneutics serve the methodology of the social sciences. Repeating his thesis on the universality of human linguisticality, he attempts to place hermeneutics beyond methodological alienation: "The *Geisteswissenschaften* were the starting-point of my analysis in *Truth and Method* precisely because they related to experiences that have nothing to do with method and science but live beyond science. . . . The hermeneutical experience is prior to all methodological alienation."[11]

The alternative, he holds, is self-reflecting activity by "controlled alienation," which he thinks will produce an alienated understanding. To Habermas' suggestion that his method offers a projected futurity without reference to any operational effectiveness, he responds that what is at issue is seeing through "the dogmatism of asserting an opposition and separation between the ongoing natural 'tradition' and the reflective appropriation of it."[12]

To Habermas' charge that he is jettisoning the heritage of idealism, that is, that science is changed by reflection and that hermeneutics must pass into a critique of ideology because the "idealism of linguisticality does not cover the concrete whole of social relationships," Gadamer replies that all such critiques are themselves linguistic acts of reflection. To the objection that certain interactions require a psychotherapeutic model of discourse because of the presence of compulsions and repressions, Gadamer, while not disputing the logic of this conception, insists that hermeneutics does not take its bearings from a limiting concept of perfect interaction between understood motives and consciously performed action.

This leads him to reject Habermas' charge that "hermeneutics bangs helplessly from within against the walls of tradition," a view that follows from assuming that cultural tradition is somehow fixed—an implication which Gadamer denies.

The linguisticality of being means that there is no primordial world of meaning behind language. For Gadamer, "being that can be understood is language." He would deny any privileged perspective to critical theory, arguing that language is not just a subject of the historical process open to observation and objectification, "rather it is by itself the game of interpretation that we are all engaged in every day. In this game nobody is above and before all the others: everybody is at the center of 'it' in this game. Thus it is always his turn to be interpreting."[13]

For Gadamer, reason does not always have to be emancipative in the sense of unmasking pretension. Authority is not always wrong. Reason and authority stand in an ambivalent rather than an antithetical relationship as the Enlightenment held. Tradition as a ground of understanding does not alter the fact that authority is rooted in insight. For Gadamer, then, nothing lies outside the scope of hermeneutics.

A Psychotherapeutic Paradigm of Discourse Governed by Emancipative Interest

Already in *Knowledge and Human Interests,* Habermas has characterized the work of Freud as being "relevant to us as the only tangible example of a science incorporating methodological self-reflection." His goal is to reconstruct psychoanalysis as a theory of distorted communication, with a view to finding guidelines for the construction of a critical social theory. Freud's initial patterning of the interpretation of dreams on the model of philological hermeneutics required development to take account of the latent content of symbolic expressions: the "internal foreign territory." Thus the psychoanalyst deals with a text that both expresses and conceals: "The meaning of a corrupt text of this sort can be comprehended only after it has been possible to illuminate the meaning of the corruption itself. This distinguishes the peculiar task of a hermeneutics that cannot be confined to the procedures of philology but rather unites linguistic analysis with the psychological investigation of casual connections."[14]

His point is that the "depth hermeneutics" that Freud developed to deal with such texts rely on theoretical perspectives and technical rules that go beyond the normal competences of a speaker of a language. In dealing with systematically distorted communication, "hermeneutic" consciousness of translation is inadequate, for the incomprehensibility results from a faulty organization of speech itself.

The analyst and the client enter into a form of communication with the aim of setting in motion a process of enlightenment and bringing the client into self-reflection. For Habermas, repression results in a privatization of semantic content that does not obey the grammatical rules of everyday language. The retranslation of this distorted semantic content requires a combination of interpretative understanding and causal explanation: "The disclosure of the meaning of specific incomprehensible acts or utterances develops to the same extent as in the course of reconstruction of the original scene, a clarification of the genesis of the faulty meaning is achieved. The What, the semantic content of a systematically distorted manifestation cannot be 'understood' if it is not possible at the same time to 'explain' The Why, the origin of the . . . systematic distortion itself."[15]

In this way, Habermas would seek to argue that in its methodological features, psychoanalysis gives us an indication of how critical theory might proceed in its task of enlightenment within dialogue.

Gadamer replies by arguing that this model may not be generalized, since its legitimacy follows from consensus within specific limitations. By neglecting those limits, he suggests, Habermas' argument will not hold.

Fundamentally, his objection is based on the conviction that any generalization of such a paradigm implies the constitution of self-appointed elites who claim a privileged access to the truth, an objection P. Berger has repeated in relation to the conscientization project of P. Freire.[16] "All social and political manifestations of will are dependent on the building up of common conviction through rhetoric. This implies . . . that one must always reckon, with the possibility that opposing convictions, whether in the individual or in the social sphere, could be right."[17]

Thus Gadamer insists on the dialogical basis of all access to truth, both theoretical and practical.

The Three Levels of Critique and Their Rational Criteria

In reply to this criticism of Gadamer as well as to those who, from a more thoroughgoing Marxist perspective,[18] argued that the psychoanalytic model of discourse was not adapted to revolutionary practice, Habermas first distinguishes three aspects of the question. These are "the formation and extension of critical theorems which can stand up to scientific discourse; the organization of processes of enlightenment in which such theorems are applied and can be tested . . . and finally the selection of appropriate strategies. . . . On the first level the aim is true statements; on the second authentic insights; and on the third prudent decisions."[19]

Our chief concern here is with the second level. For it is here that the model of communicative interaction is that of therapeutic discourse. The dialogical situation is asymmetrical. Indeed, the inability of one of the partners to participate in genuine dialogue, at least at a given stage, is a presupposition of the exercise. Habermas argues that—as in psychoanalysis—since the final authority is the client, there is a safeguard against exploitative deception.

Critical theory, in renouncing the contemplative claims of theories constructed in monologic form, understands itself as verifiable only within the process of self-enlightenment. Its therapeutic function is demanded by the distortion of communication that has occurred in the manner in which the ideal of public discourse and enlightenment, presumed to exist, at least in principle, among a public constituted by reasoning private persons, and secured in various institutional and constitutional ways, has subsequently been distorted and manipulated by the oppressive structures of contemporary societies. This distortion and manipulation is further legitimated and enforced through the mind control of the mass media.

Habermas' aim is to treat psychoanalysis as an analysis of language to show how the relations of power, embodied in systematically distorted communication, can be confronted by critique leading to emancipation from dependencies. Thus he will not allow a hermeneutical idealism that might reduce the complexes of meaning within social systems to the contents of cultural tradition: "The immunizing power of ideologies, which stifle the demands for justification raised by discursive examination, goes back to blockages in communication independent of the changing semantic contents. These blocks have their origins within the structures of communication themselves. . . . Thus they require explanation within the framework of a theory of systematically distorted communication."[20]

Habermas takes up the objection that the transference of the psychoanalytic model will lead to self-appointed elites dogmatically claiming a privileged access to truth. He begins by noting that a retracing of the ego's identity through all involutions of systematically distorted communication means only the assimilation of the structures of distortion. The problem is merely deferred. He goes on to argue that the notion of a distorted communication, as in the case of a deceptive consensus, is highly dependent upon a normative real understanding and is illustrated in real consensus attained discursively and recognizably rational. One of the reasons why the emancipative interest of knowledge exhibits itself is precisely that repression presents itself permanently in systematically distorted communication: "This interest aims at reflection on oneself. As soon as we seek to clarify the structure of this reflection within the reference system of action discourse, its difference from scientific argumentation becomes clear: the psychoanalytic dialogue is not a discourse and reflection on oneself does not provide reasoned justification. What is reasoned justification within the context of acts of reflection on oneself bases itself on theoretical knowledge which has been gained independently of the reflections on oneself, namely, the rational reconstruction of rule systems."[21]

Habermas admits that, up to then, he did not adequately distinguish these. A reliable criterion of distinction is available. What self-reflection makes conscious has new practical consequences;

rational reconstructions do not. Self-reflection effects "both more and less than discussion": less, because of the asymmetry of the dialogue; more, because it is not a discourse cut free from action or experience. It produces insight that satisfies not only a claim to discursive correctness but, in addition, a claim to authenticity.

Psychoanalysis has two fundamental and pragmatic sanctions against an exploitative misuse: first, its theoretical foundations are scientifically defensible; second, the appropriateness of the process is confirmed in self-application: "in other words the patient himself is the final authority." Habermas accepts that Gadamer is correct in criticizing any undifferentiated transference of the model to interaction between large groups. The model is transferable only to the interaction between groups seeking enlightenment and those wishing to facilitate it.

The three functions cannot be fulfilled according to the same principles. Theory requires theoretical discourse; processes of enlightenment require—in addition to proper precaution—therapeutic discourse; action demands consensus on the basis of practical discourse. Thus, a theory designed for enlightenment is tested on various levels. Its theoretically derived hypotheses can be refuted or confirmed in scientific argumentation. At this theoretical level, the validity claim, in relation to enlightenment, can only be confirmed tentatively. It can only be realized in the successful process of enlightenment leading to free acceptance. This, in turn, will remain in some sense tentative, since there will always be some who will not accept the process under any given set of circumstances.

A process of enlightenment can create a consciousness that can bring about the conditions under which systematic distortions of communication are dissolved and a practical discourse can be conducted. But, as in the case of psychoanalysis, the client draws his own conclusions for action. Self-reflection produces changes in attitude. Strategic action presupposes this. "That the stategic action of those who have decided to engage in struggle, and that means to take risks, can be interpreted hypothetically as a retrospection which is possible only in anticipation, but at the same time not compellingly justified on this level with the aid of a reflexive theory has its good reason: the vindicating superiority of those who do the enlightening over those who are to be enlightened is theoretically unavoidable, but at the same time it is fictive and requires self-correction; in a process of enlightenment there can only be participants."[22]

Final empirical verification requires universal enlightenment, for only then can discourse be held among all participants. But this cannot invalidate strategic action on the basis of this theory. Apart from the fact that it is a condition impossible to fulfill, it forgets that no authentic action is risk free.

Implications for the Present Discussion

The existence, de facto, of hermeneutically valid models of discourse where there is, in principle, an asymmetry between the mutually corrective dialogical contributions of the conversation partners indicates that all hermeneutical perspectives are not a priori equivalent. Inasmuch as theology too has its "internal foreign territory," since its rootedness in the whole gamut of human experience implies that it may, at least sometimes, exercise a superstructural function in relation to systems of oppression, the concept of "systematically distorted communication" is also applicable to it. In this case, the theory-praxis dialectic in theology requires mediation by a process of enlightenment that must necessarily be organized in a manner whereby one conversation partner has what Habermas terms "a vindicatory superiority." We must now seek to illustrate this.

Notes

[1] H.-G. Gadamer, *Wahrheit und Methode: Grundzuege einer Philosophischen Hermeneutik* (Tuebingen, 1960); English trans., *Truth and Method* (London, 1975). *See* 146, 192f., 245f. On Gadamer's rehabilitation of the hermeneutical significance of prejudice *(Vorurteile),* see *Truth and Method,* pp. 239–253.

[2] Ibid., 251; cf. also 324. From one point of view, the whole of Gadamer's work may be described as a retrieval of the importance of tradition. He writes, "The anticipation of meaning that governs our understanding of a text is not an act of subjectivity but proceeds from the communality that binds us to a tradition. . . . Tradition is not simply a precondition into which we come, but we produce it ourselves; inasmuch as we understand, we participate in the evolution of tradition and we hence further determine it ourselves" (p. 261).

[3] Ibid., 237. "My thesis is that the element of effective-history is operative in all understanding of tradition" (xxi).

[4] Ibid., 341. Cf. also 331.

[5] *Truth and Method,* 263–264. Note also the future implications: "It is part of the historical finiteness of our being, that we are aware that after us, others will understand in a different way" (p. 336).

[6] J. Habermas, *Zur Logik des Socialwissenschaften* (Frankfort, 1971). The section of this work relevant to the present discussion appears as "A review of Gadamer's *Truth and Method*" in T. McCarthy and F. Allmayr, eds., *Understanding and Social Enquiry* (South Bend, 1977) 353–363.

[7] *Truth and Method,* 346–347.

[8] "A Review of Gadamer's *Truth and Method,*" 351. For Habermas, demonstrating the interpreter's relationship to tradition is Gadamer's "real achievement."

[9] Ibid., 358, 360.

[10] Ibid, 361. Cf. also P. Ricoeur, "Habermas and Gadamer in dialogue," 162.

[11] H.-G. Gadamer, "On the Scope and Function of Hermeneutics," *Philosophical Hermeneutics* (Berkeley, 1976) 26. Cf. 18–43; *see* p. 19.

[12] Ibid., 28.

[13] Ibid., 32.

[14] *Knowledge and Human Interests* (Boston, 1971) 217. Original title, *Erkenntnis und Interesse* (Frankfort, 1966).

[15] *See* K.-O. Apel ed., *Hermeneutik und Ideologiekritik* (Frankfort, 1971), where Habermas' essay "Universalitaetsanspruch der Hermeneutik" first appeared. This is translated as "On Systematically Distorted Communication," *Inquiry* 13 (1970) 204–218. Cf. 208–209 and 205.

[16] It is interesting to note that P. Berger in *Pyramids of Sacrifice: Political Ethics and Social Change* (New York, 1974) has made a virtually identical criticism of Freire's *conscientização* project. Berger dismisses it as the "false consciousness of consciousness raising," emphasizing the "equality of all empirically available worlds of consciousness." Apart from the dubious rendering of *conscientização* by "consciousness raising" in a transitive sense and insufficient attention to the manner in which consciousness is differentiated (cf. Lonergan, *Method in Theology,* 303), Berger overlooks the fundamentally dialogical character of Freire's project. Cf. *Pedagogy of the Oppressed,* 60f. Besides, the fact that those working for transformation have a project in mind no more takes from the dialogical character of their enterprises than do "prejudices" in the Gadamerian sense from hermeneutical conversation. On the contrary, self-critical commitment is actually a condition of the possibility of dialogue. On the falsity of "irenism" in dialogue, *see* SPnC, *Dialogue with Non-Believers* (Vatican, 1968) 29.

[17] Gadamer, *Replik, Continuum* 8 (1970) 316–317.

[18] While in the hermeneutics debate, Habermas is seen by the Gadamerians as compromising its conversational nature, by Marxists he is seen as reducing the revolution to dialogue. Cf. *Western Marxism,* 163f.

[19] *Theory and Practice,* 32.

[20] Ibid., 12.

[21] Ibid., 22.

[22] Ibid., 30.

10

The Relative Normative Status of the Hermeneutical Privilege of the Poor

Having emphasized the importance of the question as to whether the preferential option for the poor furnishes theology with a privileged hermeneutical perspective, we illustrated how this methodological perspective was operative in the work of five important contemporary theologians. At that stage, we noted the lack of consensus as to the methodological status of this approach, not to mention how this status might be established. By considering the principal lines of critique of this method, we argued that it emerges as a valid and important expression of Catholic theology. It was clear, however, that it needed to modify its occasional claim to be a totally new theology, as well as any pretension to an absolute hermeneutical privilege, given the dialogical nature of theological conversation. Before attempting to establish the principal methodological foundations of the proposed theological optic, we spelled out, as fully as possible, what the option for the poor actually means for the theologian. We returned then to the scriptural core of the tradition, where we find a compelling prima facie argument for the interpretative privilege of the poor, noting that we could have stopped there were it not for the appeal to the dialogical nature of theological conversation, which seeks to rule out a priori any case for a hermeneutical privilege. In the light of our interpretation of the Gadamer-Habermas debate, we will now seek to indicate how a theology, elaborated out of solidarity with the poor and marginalized, exercises a hermeneutical privilege in its methodological conversation with other theologies and thereby possesses a relative normative methodological status.

The Tradition and the Option for the Poor: A Fusing of Horizons

The unmasking of the Enlightenment's "prejudice against prejudice" allows a preferential option for the poor to be consciously employed as an "initial directedness of our whole ability to experience" and therefore to reflect theologically. Theology is at last delivered from some putative neutralized stance that would allegedly guarantee objectivity. The "fusion of horizons" *(Horizontsversmeltzung)* between the horizon of this option and that of the tradition, realized in the praxis of the theologian, then allows the disclosure of a new range of meanings as Gutiérrez, and latterly, *Libertatis conscientia,* intimated. In this fusion of horizons, "something new comes to be." It is neither the immediate awareness, with less-differentiated consciousness, of the poor themselves nor the detached objectified information of the academic. In the active reciprocity of their dialogue, they "do not remain what (they) were." In becoming "bound to one another in a new community," this "transformation into a communion" allows a discourse to emerge that, on the one hand, is truly "good news for the poor," and on the other, is a new phase in methodological self-appropriation on the part of the theological tradition. The "circle of the unexpressed" around earlier phases of the tradition comes to more complete expression. Because meaning is always codetermined by the situation of the interpreter, the option for the poor becomes less a thematic than an actual horizon of understanding.

However, because the same process of hermeneutical conversation is also underway in function of other interpretative frameworks as well as between them, a theology from the perspective of an option for the poor might seem, to one point of view, to be just one conversation partner among many in the ensuing dialogue, which could not, in principle, claim any hermeneutical privilege. This, as we have seen, is essentially the position of Tracy.

The Critical Function of the Option for the Poor

The fact that *subtilitas applicandi* is constitutive of interpretative understanding implies that theological understanding is necessarily rooted in and directed toward agapeistic action in the world. This raises a caveat in the face of the theoretically true principle that theological understanding can never extricate itself from its previous history. It questions any restrictive understanding of the manner in which submission to the theological tradition—which did not and does not always operate from the perspective of the option of the poor—is a condition of theological self-awareness.

Theology from the perspective of the poor would have serious reservations about what seems to be a subordination in principle of any new praxis-linked interpretation to "the profound movement of tradition." Tradition, as understood at any given period in its history, including today, cannot be construed as an interpretative *ne plus ultra;* but precisely to continue as "the Tradition," it must be open to possible profound alteration.[1] The theological option being explored here would not hesitate to unmask and seek to eliminate any element of the theological tradition's authority that might more properly be called domination.

An unself-critical aspect of the ecclesiastical structure can seek to legitimate itself theologically—thus endangering the credibility of theology as a science—unless theological self-awareness is linked to social analysis and a sociology of theology. Tradition in this limiting sense is surpassable; otherwise we risk reducing theology to a state of historical inefficacy, if not undermining it altogether in fundamentalism.

The Scope of the Theological Tradition

Theological hermeneutics also has a universal scope because everything that can be understood, can be understood theologically. Therefore, the theological tradition finds itself recognizing the questions raised by the relationship of theology to the social sciences. In doing so, of course, theology refuses to allow its methodology to be determined by that of a science with a different formal object.

In seeking to transcend the possibility of methodological alienation, theology can, however, be doing one of two very different things. First, it can be seeking to genuinely expand its interpretative horizons and evolve new nuances of method. Second, it might be only notionally committed to this and be—consciously or unconsciously—seeking to resolve the new problematic within the old *Fragestellung* and thus ultimately blunting, if not eliminating, the significance of the new question. Certainly, any theological critique of theological method remains a theological discourse. But if understood in the sense of permanently debarring any *nouvelle theologie,* we are dealing then with an understanding of theological method that "bangs helplessly from within the walls of tradition."

Yet to the follower of Gadamer, a theological tradition that would overcome this limitation, precisely because it is self-reforming, would seek to deny any privileged hermeneutical status to the option for the poor—or to any other perspective in theology. In order to remain theology, a theological critique cannot exit from the theological dialogue. For theology, too, critique and tradition would stand in an ambivalent rather than an antithetical relationship, and in that sense the theological tradition would remain the ground of theological understanding.

Theological Method as Self-enlightenment of Theology

A contemporary theological method, if it is to sustain the claim to being methodic and scientific, must, in a post-Modern era, incorporate methodological self-reflection. One of the corollaries of a theological perspective privileging the poor is to point to the "internal foreign territory" of theology. Methodological self-awareness cannot accept that theological texts are solely and always revelatory of God—they can also be superstructural justifying statements of "the systematic distortion" of the will of God in situations of inhumanity. In theology, too, there may be "systematically distorted communication."[2] Psychologists and spiritual directors are familiar with the situation in which a veneer of religious language possesses a fundamentally pathological character distorting communication and intensifying some internalized oppression. Critical theologians can recognize an analogous pattern in some expressions of the theological tradition—without thereby going to the unwarranted extreme of denouncing the tradition as such.

Quite clearly, the distortion of theological language may not be confined to individuals. It really does enter and codetermine the tradition.[3] Thus, the consciousness of *ecclesia semper reformanda*[4] in the Church cannot appeal to a "Holy Church" over against a "sinful people of God." In relation to the real holiness of the Church, the question must be asked "in a really radical and explicit way, whether and to what extent her 'objective,' 'institutional' holiness, in teaching, sacrament and law suffer a kind of reaction from the sinfulness of her members, if these realities are viewed not merely in abstraction but in their historical reality and in their actual realization by human beings in the Church."[5]

Following Habermas' introduction of the psychoanalytic paradigm, we may, in espousing a critical theology, and in particular, theology from the perspective of the poor, point to a situation that cannot be dealt with using normal theological linguistic competence. Instead, a recognition of systematically distorted communication in theology itself is called for. This implies a form of theological dialogue that invokes a conscious process of enlightenment, aimed at dissolving the content of the distorted theological discourse through uncovering its irrational roots in pathological human structures, for which aspects of the theological tradition may serve as an unconscious legitimation.

For many commentators, there will be an instinctive unreadiness to generalize from a psychoanalytic model with its inevitable limitations. Some theologians would balk at the apparent suggestion that their guild could be divided into those who were or who were not the *alombrados,* especially if the former appear to be a self-appointed elite claiming a privileged perspective on the truth.

Paradoxically, the theological tradition has itself frequently assigned greater relative normative status to some theologies as well as an a priori privilege of perspective—notably to the magisterium.[6] It has been demonstrated that the concept of magisterium is itself something that has undergone considerable development and is, in principle, capable of further development.[7] Not only does this seem to preclude any a priori dismissal of the possibility of a privileged hermeneutical standpoint in theology, but it points the debate in the direction of what that perspective might be. In particular, it raises the important question of defining the evangelical, and therefore the theological, relationship between the magisterium of the Church and the experience and perspective of the poor.

Nonetheless, in terms of the ministry of intellectual service of the faith, it is crucial to defend the principle of the dialogical basis of access to truth both at the theoretical and practical levels. This would imply that the theologian, who through an option for the poor embraces their perspective, allows the possibility that other perspectives on theology would also have their own claims to validity, to be explored in an ongoing theological conversation.

The Hidden Preference in the Conversational Model

In Tracy's brilliant espousal of the Gadamerian position on hermeneutics, he has made a strong case for the conversational paradigm of theological method to the exclusion of any hermeneutical privilege for any theological perspective, including one from the perspective of the poor. His approach, however, raises two important questions. The first asks whether this is a real resolution of the question or a merely conceptual one. The second asks if there is not already a tacit preference for the academic-rhetorical-traditional over the practical-critical-transformational in the way in which both the question and the response are couched. Moreover, he does not seem to have allowed his own observation that Gadamer's achievement is "in danger of becoming an unconsciously retrospective Utopia" by remaining "insufficiently sensitive to ideology critique,"[8] to have sufficiently influenced his own hermeneutical model.

Is not the subsequently elaborated notion of theological conversation a rather subtle manner—even if unconsciously so—of reinforcing a preference for the theology of the academy? For in attempting to discuss the relative claims of the three theologies to methodological priority, it seems clear that the metatheological discussion is itself addressed primarily to the academy and therefore remains within the context of the latter's problematic, and thus implicitly favors its perspective. As Lamb has observed, Tracy's attempt to distinguish the complementarity of the three theological disciplines remains within foundational theology.[9] For Tracy, foundational theology answers primarily to the academy. Certainly, no discussion on theological method can sacrifice academic rigor and to that extent must remain an academic work.

But the point at issue is whether it is driven to this necessary degree of theoretical rigor primarily in function of an evangelical commitment to love as served by truth, or primarily in function of a scientific norm implicit in the ethos of a given academy, with an often tacit support for existing structures of power and privilege—especially when such structures remain unexamined.

Sobrino's juxtapositioning of the "bar of reason" and the "yearning for transformation," though simplistic insofar as the two cannot be dichotomized, is still instructive. Clearly, any serious theological enterprise, especially one concerned with method, must be justified before the "bar of reason." But just as theory is an inner moment in praxis, which is both more primordial and more ultimate, so is theological method's justification at the bar of reason an inner moment in its justification before the yearning for transformation.

The Three Levels of Theological Conversation

In order to understand at what level of discourse the present work argues for a hermeneutical privilege in theology in respect of an option for the poor, we shall first seek to apply Habermas' three levels of critique, as well as their criteria, to theological method.

1. At the level of the formation and extension of theological data, the model is scientific discourse aiming at truth-statements. The criteria here are scholarship, logical coherence, and coherence with the tradition. At this level, the option for the poor can claim no hermeneutical privilege except in an indirect way by posing fundamental questions that might be otherwise overlooked. But in the actual dialogue on the question, the hermeneutical perspective per se does not guarantee a superior theoretical performance.

2. At the level of evangelical strategy, the theologians operating from the perspective of the poor have no a priori privilege inasmuch as the model of discourse is that of reaching consensus or reaching prudent decisions. Here they are equal partners in the search for consensus. The only difference is again an indirect one in that the perspective adopted will point the Christian community in the direction of actions and strategies often overlooked. It would not, however, grant any privilege in actually reaching

a consensus for action. An evangelical option for the poor would not necessarily guarantee prudence in decision making.

3. It is at the second level that the question of a hermeneutical privilege arises in a direct way. Although theological theory elaborated from the perspective of the poor continues to need as well as provide amplification and critical correction from theologies elaborated from the other perspectives, nevertheless there is an inescapable asymmetry in the dialogue. For this hermeneutic attempts theology from the perspective of God's own chosen ones; therefore, within the limits of any human discourse, it is relatively free from the particular form of systematically distorted communication that besets theology: that of providing a legitimation mechanism for the existing social structures.

Thus, the privilege of the perspective of the poor operates neither at the level of theory nor at the level of practice—when these are understood in the narrower sense—but precisely at their interface. In the dialogue between the theology elaborated from this perspective and that elaborated from another, there is, assuming an equivalence of theoretical performance, a mutual growth in awareness in respect of the practical roots of their respective hermeneutical standpoints. Whereas each will grow in awareness of the various limitations, compulsions, biases, and oversights that beset any intellectual inquiry and always call for intellectual conversion on the part of the theologian, nevertheless, the fundamental asymmetry remains. For, in principle, the limitations just alluded to apply equally to all concerned, whereas at the other level, that is, becoming methodologically self-conscious in respect of the social roots and destination of one's theology, there is an unbridgeable asymmetry. For whereas some theological enterprises have their roots in the aspirations of the poor and suffering, others have their roots in legitimating a variety of structures, which, in varying degrees and to different extents, are allied to existing structures of power and oppression. It is at this level of the mutual enlightenment that a theological method operating—truly and not just notionally—with the option for the poor as its hermeneutical perspective can claim a methodological privilege.

Needless to say, while these three levels are distinct, they are also interdependent. The degree of methodological self-awareness reached through entry into a self-critical emancipative process at the second level may—as indicated—have a dramatic effect on the choice of thematic at the first level and of strategy at the third. In this way, adopting the hermeneutical standpoint of the poor— in addition to creating conditions for theology's methodological self-enlightenment—would also effect both the internal "autonomous" forum of theological theory as well as Christian praxis in the world.

The dialogical character of the process is safeguarded inasmuch as those who participate will ultimately choose their own way of doing theology. The specific point at issue cannot be argued in theoretical terms beyond this degree of certainty—something that does not differentiate it from many fundamental theological issues, including the act of faith itself. A final verification can only be arrived at by participating in the process of therapeutic methodological enlightenment outlined. To the extent that this might be seen as indicating a reduced degree of verification, it discloses just how far reason has been instrumentalized and cut off from its roots in praxis.

Without consciously entering this "internal foreign territory," theological method risks legitimating the current relations of power and marginalization, whose reflection can be found in some religious language. To the degree that it declines to recognize the extent to which theological language can be systematically distorted, it moves closer to the rock upon which theology, and ultimately religion itself, would perish: that rock of pseudostability that is merely a legitimation of the way things are.

The Relative Normative Status of the Option for the Poor as a Hermeneutical Perspective in Contemporary Catholic Theology

If the scope of hermeneutics is universal, then it includes models of discourse that, because of their avowedly therapeutic function and goal, imply an unavoidable asymmetry in the dialogue. The existence of systematically distorted communication in theology implies that here too there are methodological dialogues with an asymmetry between the partners. Since the Church is also the Church of sinners, the theological traditions that articulate the Church's self-awareness cannot be presumed a priori to be totally free from distortions. In maintaining the reflex character of the relation between theory and praxis, it is not possible to maintain the dogmatic truth of practical sin in the Church while arguing for an a priori impeccability in its theory. This, at the theoretical level, no more impugns the doctrine of the inerrancy of revelation and its transmission than the doctrine of the Church of sinners does that of the indefectibility of the Church at the practical level. If *ecclesia semper reformanda* is a theological principle, then it is a principle that applies to theological method itself, and clearly *reformanda* implies much more than development. It points to methodological correction through self-enlightenment, which is the methodological analogue of conversion.

It is here that the hermeneutical privilege of the poor becomes apparent. For that process of methodological self-correction, which the theologian undergoes through his or her own genuine conversion to the poor, becomes a privileged perspective from which, albeit within the ongoing theological conversation, the always necessary methodological self-enlightenment of theological method proceeds. Having undergone this process, which is equally one of conversion and methodological enlightenment, the theologian operating from the resultant hermeneutical perspective can now facilitate a similar process in the theological conversation. This is why it necessarily requires a real and actual option for the poor on his or her part.

It also indicates why only a relatively complete degree of verification of the theory being elaborated here is possible without the conversation partner entering consciously into the very process of enlightenment, which itself leads to a preferential option for the poor. But by the same token, it also indicates that any demand for the absolute theoretical verification of a theological theorem misunderstands the practical roots and goals of theology and therefore the nature of theology itself.

Thus, the hermeneutical privilege of the option for the poor in theological method is not an ethical privilege, nor even an analytical one in terms of theory or praxis considered in themselves. Its privilege lies in the fact that it is the irreplaceable perspective from which theology can critically correct its methodological self-awareness. In essence, it does this by exercising a therapeutic role, whereby it creates conditions for theologians to come to an awareness of the practical roots of their models of discourse. In turn, they discover whether or not that practical rootedness truly favors that new quality of human solidarity which is both the expression and the anticipation of the kingdom of God—present "already and not yet"—and without which, the meaning of creation —humankind's being in the image and likeness of God—can never be visible.

Notes

[1] The most obvious contemporary example of the inability to see this is the schismatic movement begun by the late M. Lefebvre.

[2] A complete discussion of the details of systematically distorted communication in theology would take us beyond the scope of the present discussion: here a schematic indication of such a discussion is offered. Consider, e.g., the psuedolegitimation of apartheid in the Dutch Reformed Church, or—although self-criticism is always more difficult in one's own tradition—we might, with the objectivity afforded by the centuries, examine the preaching of the Crusades, the Inquisition—or some aspects of it— as well as the legitimation of the Conquistadores and examine how in each case there occurred a systematic distortion of theological language. Note, not just distortions in the language in some occasional sense but systematic distortion with an actual grammar.

The contemporary example receiving most attention is, of course, the distortion of theological communication stemming from an excessively patriarchal Church and academy.

[3] "Such devaluation, distortion, dilution, corruption may occur only in scattered individuals. But it may occur on a more massive scale, and then the words are repeated but the meaning is gone. The chair remains the chair of Moses, but occupied by the Scribes and Pharisees; The theology is still Scholastic, but the Scholasticism is decadent. . . . So the unauthenticity of individuals becomes the unauthenticity affecting a tradition." (Lonergan, *A Third Collection*, 213).

[4] Vatican II's call to the Church for a *perennis reformatio* in *Unitatis redintegratio*, n. 6, may be taken as equivalent to *Ecclesia semper reformanda*. J. Feiner writes, "The consciousness that this was in fact an ancient Catholic idea was revived only in the years preceding the Council . . . but it derives from an ancient Catholic tradition. Popes, Councils and Churchmen of the Middle Ages and the Reformation period used the expression quite naturally for the Catholic Church and so did the Council of Trent." "Commentary on the Decree *Unitatis redintegratio*," in H. Vorgrimmler ed., *Commentary on the Documents of Vatican II* (New York, 1968) 4:57–162; cf. esp. pp. 95–96.

[5] K. Rahner, "The Sinful Church in the Decrees of Vatican II," TI 6, pp. 270–294; cf. esp. p. 277. Note Rahner's references to the Council of Constance (p. 270) and his refusal to allow the "Church" to be hypostasized "over against the People of God" (pp. 277, 278, 284).

[6] If there is a reflex relationship between theory and praxis and if sinfulness in the Church is in the institution through being in the members, then apart from the infallible exercise of the extraordinary magisterium, one cannot rule out absolutely and a priori the possibility, in certain circumstances, of distortions of theological language either in the exercise or in the understanding of the magisterium. As one possible illustration of this, consider certain aspects of the Modernist crisis. Cf. G. Daly, *Transcendence and Immanence: A Study in Catholic Modernism and Integralism* (Oxford, 1980), esp. pp. 190–207, "The Integralist Response: Pascendi and After"; *see also* P. Hebblethwaite, *John XXIII* (London, 1985) 49–75.

⁷*See* Y. Congar, "Bref historique des formes du 'magistère' et de ses relations avec les docteurs" RSPT 60 (1976) 99–112. Note especially his discussions of the constitution of the Council of Constance and the understanding of theology in *Humani generis*. For a full-length study of this question see F. Sullivan, *Magisterium: Teaching Authority in the Catholic Church* (Dublin, 1985); *see also* A. Lorscheider, "The Re-defined Role of the Bishop in a Poor, Religious People," Con 176:6 (1984) 47–49.

⁸*Analogical Imagination,* 137, n. 16.

⁹In *Solidarity with Victims,* Lamb goes on to say "To what extent are Tracy's distinctions . . . immunizing the discipline of foundations and systematics against the claims of liberation. . . . I suspect his analysis . . . remains inadequate on this issue" (p. 81); cf. *Analogical Imagination,* 62–64.

Conclusions

We may now proceed, by way of conclusion, to sum up the results of our investigations in the following theses:

1. A theology from the perspective of the option for the poor is the thematization of the fundamental salvific truth that the God revealed in the Judeo-Christian tradition identifies himself with the weak, the oppressed, and the crucified.

2. A theology from the perspective of the option for the poor is constitutive of Christian theology, because this latter cannot simply be a theology about the poor or for the poor. A genuinely dialogical *koinōnia* in the struggle of the poor implies a fusion of interpretative horizons between this perspective and that of the theological tradition.

3. In this fusion of horizons something new comes to be. What emerges is no longer either an immediate experience with undifferentiated consciousness nor an objectified but conceptual-notional grasp of the question. The horizon of understanding that emerges truly reveals the gospel as good news to the poor and coextensively represents a new stage in the methodological self-appropriation of the tradition.

4. The massive catastrophic suffering of whole peoples in poverty and marginalization is more than a theological theme. Since salvation in Jesus Christ is historically mediated through the achievement of a new quality of human solidarity of which the poor are the privileged architects, involvement in the struggle of the poor is a condition of the lived faith, which seeks self-understanding in theology.

5. The dimensions of the Christian faith that emerge as a consequence of theologizing from the perspective of the option for the poor are constitutive of the essence of that faith and not merely additional developments.

6. While liberation theology from the perspective of the option for the poor is the most pertinent and faith-enriching example of contemporary contextualized theology, it is more than this. For the fundamental significance of the poor in God's plan of salvation implies that the perspective of the option for the poor is a quasi-invariant methodological principle in theology.

7. Theology from the perspective of the option for the poor necessarily involves socioanalytical hermeneutical mediation with a self-critical ideological dimension; since it employs this in a theological *Aufhebung*, what is articulated is not ideology but theology.

8. Acquiring the perspective of the poor is not an additional theological datum but an existential transformation of the reality that the theologian is, with the fourfold dimension of evangelical simplicity, existential solidarity with the poor, the employment of transformational socioanalytical mediation, and self-critical institutional involvement.

9. The acquisition of the perspective of the option for the poor is not a substitute for theoretical rigor in theology but, rather, is theological theory's practical rootedness and goal. Theology from the perspective of the option for the poor may not permit itself a lesser theoretical rigor than "academic" theology. However, its self-justification before the "bar of reason" is rooted in a more primordial self-justification before the yearning of the poor for a transformed world, which is itself a privileged locus for grasping the salvific will of God.

10. As intellectual, moral, and religious conversion are foundational of the reality that the theologian is, and as conversion to a genuinely dialogical participation in the life of the poor is fundamental to Christian conversion, so the preferential option for the poor is foundational of genuinely Christian theological method.

11. Since the option for the poor, like any sociopolitical rootedness, is finite and limited, a theology from the perspective of this option is not the whole of theology but a limited though relatively normative and privileged hermeneutical standpoint. While it expands the methodological self-awareness of existing theology in an unparalleled manner, it remains organically linked to the tradition.

12. Theology from the perspective of an option for the poor remains a conversation partner with theologies elaborated from the other hermeneutical perspectives. It denies, however, that the nature of this theological conversation can be properly ascertained in an investigation that answers primarily to an academic ethos without inquiring into the implicit sociopolitical interests of that ethos.

13. Each theological perspective, in being a dialogue partner, is, in principle, both a provider and a recipient of enrichment and critical correction to and from other theological perspectives. In relation to theology from the perspective of the option for the poor, however, this mutually enriching and corrective dialogue is asymmetrical.

14. Theology from the perspective of the option for the poor does not claim direct hermeneutical privilege at the level of theoretical rigor except insofar as it furnishes fundamental themes in a manner that would otherwise be overlooked.

15. Theology from the perspective of the option for the poor claims no direct hermeneutical privilege in the process of deciding on the exigencies of Christian action in the world except insofar as it focuses on areas of action that are rarely given their true importance.

16. The hermeneutical privilege of the option for the poor in theology consists directly in its therapeutic function, in relation to all other theological perspectives, in that it creates for them conditions for a discovery of methodological self-awareness in relation to their own unobjectified sociopolitical rootedness and destination and their possible relatedness to structures of oppression.

17. In relation to the other therapeutic functions of theological dialogue, theology from the perspective of the option for the poor is, in principle, no greater nor lesser a recipient than any other theology. But in relation to the systematic distortion of theological language and conceptualization due to the—usually unconscious—rootedness of aspects of theological reflection in structures of privilege and oppression, its therapeutic role is privileged.

18. The hermeneutical privilege of a theology elaborated from the perspective of the option for the poor consists specifically in its capacity to create conditions for other theological perspectives

to become conscious of the relation between the practical roots and goals of their theological perspectives and the structural causes of poverty and oppression—and to correct the consequences.

19. The asymmetry of this therapeutic dialogue implies a hermeneutical privilege for the conversational perspective that facilitates this self-enlightenment process, that is, the perspective afforded by the option for the poor.

20. To this extent and within these limits, the option for the poor furnishes Christian theology with a privileged hermeneutical perspective.

Select Bibliography

Boff, C. *Theology and Praxis* (New York, 1987)

Boff, L. *A Fé na Periferia do Mundo* (Petropolis, 1978)

_____. *Church: Charism and Power* (London, 1983)

_____. *Jesus Christ Liberator* (London, 1980)

_____. *Teologia do Cativeiro e da Libertação* (Petropolis, 1976)

CDF *Libertius nuntius* (Vatican, 1984)

_____. *Libertatis conscientiae* (Vatican, 1986)

Congar, Y. *The Tradition and the Traditions* (London, 1962)

Dupont, J. *Les Béatitudes* 3 vols. vol. 1 (Lovain, 1954) vols. 2 and 3 (Paris, 1969)

Gadamer, H.-G. *Truth and Method* (London, 1975)

_____. *Philosophical Hermeneutics* (Berkeley, 1975)

Gutiérrez-Merino, G. *A Theology of Liberation* (New York, 1973)

_____. *We Drink from Our Own Wells* (New York, 1985)

_____. *The Power of the Poor in History* (New York, 1983)

Gutiérrez, J. *The New Libertarian Gospel: The Pitfalls of Liberation Theology* (Chicago, 1978)

Habermas, J. *Knowledge and Human Interests* (Boston, 1971)

_____. *Theory and Practice* (London, 1974)

_____. "Systematically Distorted Communication," *Inquiry* 13 (1970) 205–218

Kolakowski, L. *Main Currents of Marxism* 3 vols. (Oxford, 1973)

Lamb, M. *Solidarity with Victims* (New York, 1982)

Lonergan, B. J. F. *Method in Theology* (London, 1970)

Metz, J. B. *Followers of Christ* (London, 1978)

_____. *Faith in History and in Society* (London, 1980)

_____. *The Emergent Church* (London, 1982)

_____. *Theology of the World* (London, 1970)

Schreiter, R. *Constructing Local Theologies* (New York, 1985)

Segundo J. L. *Theology for the Artisans of a New Humanity* 5 vols. (New York, 1973f.)

_____. *The Liberation of Theology* (Dublin, 1977)

_____. *Jesus Christ: Yesterday and To-day* vols. 1, 2, and 3 (New York, 1983f.)

Sobrino, J. *Christology at the Crossroads* (London, 1978)

_____. *The True Church of the Poor* (London, 1980)

_____. *Jesus in Latin America* (New York, 1987)

Tracy, D. *Analogical Imagination: Christian Theology in the Culture of Pluralism* (London, 1981)